SEEDS OF CHANGE

STORIES OF IDB INNOVATION
IN LATIN AMERICA

By
FRANK MEISSNER

with
NANCY MORRISON

Published by the Inter-American Development Bank
Distributed by The Johns Hopkins University Press

1991
Washington, D.C.

The views and opinions expressed in this publication are those of the author and do not necessarily reflect the official position of the Inter-American Development Bank.

Seeds of Change

Stories of IDB Innovation in Latin America

Inter-American Development Bank
1300 New York Avenue, N.W.
Washington, D.C. 20577

Distributed by
The Johns Hopkins University Press
701 West 40th Street
Baltimore, Maryland 21211

ISBN: 0-940602-39-3

TABLE OF CONTENTS

LIKE A BEAUTIFUL ROSE,
SO TOO THE TRUTH HAS THORNS.

FOREWORD

BY JULIO LUNA[1]

In the early 1970s, the world witnessed what might be called the suspension of Malthus' law, the grim 18th century prediction that population growth would eventually outstrip the world's food supply. By 1977, world cereal production was seven percent higher than required for each person on the planet to obtain an adequate number of calories. Today, that production surplus has increased even further, despite world population growth.

Nonetheless, of the more than five billion people living today, over one billion suffer from different degrees of malnutrition or hunger, due to the uneven distribution of income in many countries. Food experts and national authorities are aware of this—and yet, instead of organizing a distribution system to provide all people with the food they need, a "food chain of affluence" has been created. Grain that is not eaten by people, either because they have more than they can eat or because they are too poor to buy it, is "recycled" into animal feed. The animals, in turn, are used to feed the high-income population.

About 70 percent of the cereal grains produced in industrialized countries and 40 percent of total world cereal production are processed into animal feed. Thirty percent of fish, the main and cheapest source of animal protein, is plowed back into animal feed, mainly for poultry and hogs.

The same trend exists in all nations, rich and poor, regardless of whether they have free markets or operate through centrally planned economies. In all of them, meat consumption increases as individual income rises. This paradox should cause experts and political leaders to seriously rethink food policies in the immediate future. Agricultural incentives and subsidies in the industrialized world have created surpluses. The surpluses have resulted in falling prices that affect the production of less developed agricultural countries and heighten the problems of malnutrition.

---

[1] Coordinator of Inter-Institutional Relations for the Inter-American Institute for Cooperation on Agriculture (IICA) and former Chief of the IDB's Agriculture, Fishery and Forestry Development Division.

The "food chain of affluence" is an example of how technologies for producing, preserving and distributing foods are increasingly geared to higher income markets. Rising incomes do not necessarily increase the demand for food, since no one can eat lunch or dinner several times a day. When incomes rise significantly, especially among middle and high income groups, demand for food grows not so much in quantity as in sophistication, quality and taste preferences. The "food chain of affluence" pointedly directs increased production to higher income consumers.

This distortion points to a dual set of challenges for world agricultural development. First, a new food chain is needed to make adequate foods available in sufficient quantities, provide food at the time it is needed, and give the entire population access to this food, all on a sustainable basis. Second, technologies are needed to produce, process and market farm products, based on the comparative advantages of countries, without the distortions caused by political subsidies.

In addition to meeting basic nutritional needs, the agricultural sector in Latin America has a strategic role to play in the economic reactivation of many countries affected by the current economic crisis. Agriculture on average accounts for 12 percent of the gross regional product, employs a third of the Latin American population, and accounts for nearly a third of the region's total exports. However, in most Latin American countries the agricultural sector has not lived up to its potential and comparative advantages.

The role of agriculture is all the more important because of the growing migration to the cities in many countries. By the year 2000, Latin America's population will have swelled to nearly 600 million people, 420 million of whom will live in urban areas. This creates the dual effect of reducing farm labor while increasing the demand for food, employment and basic services in the cities. Moreover, in many countries the rural population is under-employed or unemployed because of small land holdings, poor soil, or the loss of jobs through mechanization.

In most Latin American countries, modern technological advances and support services such as extension, research and credit reach only a few producers. Healthy incentives that promote fresh private investment in the agricultural sector are clearly needed. Thanks to just such effective incentives, soundly structured private fishing and forest industries have been built up in a number of Latin American countries. Some similar successes have been recorded in the modernization of grain, soybean, fruit and vegetable production.

Marketing systems and agro-industrial capacity have failed to keep pace with growing urban demand and the need to diversify farm exports. Too high a percentage of valuable export products of many Latin American countries is lost each year due to poor storage, defective packing, late shipping or rejection in the country of destination because quality controls were not strict enough or the product was improperly treated, packed or canned. Bureaucratic complications frequently help stall development in this area as well.

Clearly, there are two key long-term solutions to exploiting Latin America's comparative advantage: increased agricultural productivity and effective distribution at low cost. But these require investments in fixed capital and in technologies tailored to each country's circumstances. This in turn assigns key roles to agricultural research and technological progress. In South America, which contains the region's major agricultural countries, only 15 percent of the total cultivatable land (about 819 million hectares) is being farmed using methods even remotely as sophisticated as the modern agricultural technologies available.

More than just money is needed. In order to successfully create and adapt new technologies, people must be convinced that new ways of doing things are better than traditional methods. Moreover, agricultural technology should extend beyond the primary production cycle that ends with the harvest. It must encompass all the stages that lead the product to the consumer. Imaginative new uses for key raw materials are needed to gain access to more stable markets. Infrastructure, the marketing system, and agro-industrial processing must be developed hand-in-hand with improvements in crop production, fisheries, animal husbandry and forestry.

The 1990s usher in a new period in the development of Latin American agriculture with a clear but considerable challenge: if the sector is to help cushion the foreign debt crisis and play a major role in long-term development, the region's agriculture must be modernized. This will require an intensive process of generating and adopting technologies, applying research, and supporting rural development that actively involves beneficiaries and promotes sustainable farming. Yet the region has limited investment resources and the urgent need for foreign currency. These constraints are resulting in fewer large infrastructure projects that take time to mature. Instead, investments in more dynamic critical areas are being emphasized to make full and optimum use of current production capacity. Measures include rehabilitating irrigation infrastructure, boosting the capacity to generate and disseminate technology, developing modern marketing and quality control systems, expanding agro-industry, modernizing the physical production structure in farming, forestry and fisheries, providing ready credit, and improving mechanisms to encourage producers to save and invest.

The total investment required for Latin America's agricultural development between 1983-2000 will be $325.5 billion, according to the United Nations Food and Agriculture Organization. Investments in transportation and agro-industry will add another $100 billion, bringing the total investment required in agriculture over the period to $425.5 billion (not including rural infrastructure, fisheries or forestry). At these levels, an overall average investment of $25 billion a year in agricultural activities alone will be needed in the 1990s.

Development institutions such as the Inter-American Development Bank (IDB) will share in this investment. Since it pioneered the financing of agriculture projects by multilateral development banks in 1961, the IDB has provided some 460 loans totaling nearly $10 billion—over 20 percent of its total lending—for agriculture, forestry and fisheries projects. When combined with other financing, the cost of these projects has totalled $30 billion.

Quantifiable results, however, are only part of the real impact of these projects. In most projects, the results differed from the goals originally proposed, sometimes surpassing them and sometimes falling short. Execution frequently differed from what had been programmed. This is to be expected: human beings program and prepare, but in the end, they must bow to the imponderable ways of nature and people—droughts, floods, pests, over-production, storms, or the unexpected migration of the rural population. To these factors must be added the unforeseeable political changes that are common in developing nations, where the cultural and socio-economic dynamics of the population alter expectations and positions over very short time spans.

Often the most valuable of the IDB's contributions is the catalytic effect of its operations. In Mexico, for example, major Bank loans have been the chief source of external financing for fisheries development over the last 20 years. When the first project began, Mexico produced 350,000 tons of fish a year. By the start of the second project in 1980, production had almost tripled and by the end of the second stage in 1988, it had quintupled. How much of this achievement can be directly or indirectly attributed to IDB projects, or to the new institutions that were set up in conjunction with these projects, or to the modern business class that took over the process of expanding production? The answer is difficult to pinpoint.

To spread the benefits of improved agriculture during the 1990s and into the next century, development institutions will have to set new priorities and use new methods. There is a need, for example, to finance food inputs as part of forming "human capital", an essential objective of all development programs. Development institutions and the countries they serve must be more creative in identifying, designing and preparing projects, seeking out new areas for investment, and devising more flexible models of operation.

One point of departure would be a comprehensive socioeconomic approach in which prospective projects spring from the conclusion of diagnoses rather than from a predetermined objective. Moreover, sectoral and subsectoral investment programs should be prepared on a national and subregional scale and support countries in redesigning and adapting their policies and institutional procedures.

Some long-term programs should be financed in successive stages, under well-defined policies that favor a solid, long-term institutional commitment for support. This method is particularly effective for research programs, reforestation, storage and marketing systems, animal health and irrigation works.

Credit programs should be aimed at increasing productivity through new technologies, and should allow financing for foreign inputs (seed, fertilizer, storage, freight, insurance) to promote nontraditional exports. Initiatives are needed to attract a clientele of new agricultural entrepreneurs through mechanisms that make it possible to directly serve the private farmer. Financing criteria for recurrent costs and inputs must be flexible. They must be based on the intrinsic merits of a project and its potential contribution to satisfying basic needs and resolving the most pressing problems of the national economy.

In all of this, we cannot lose sight of the fact that multilateral development institutions are not supra-national entities. They support projects in developing countries, but in the final analysis, policies, priorities and goals are the sovereign right and responsibility of each government. In addition, on the vast canvas on which all of these efforts are displayed, neither the IDB nor any other development institution can presume to do it all with its own resources. A massive effort of coordination and cooperation must be mounted by international, regional and nongovernmental agencies for preinvestment activities, the co-financing of projects, and technical assistance needed for such ventures. Comprehensive agreements among development institutions, public and private, are the key to the future of international cooperation.

Such cooperation can be difficult in light of complex political relations among governments and multilateral institutions, and because of the diversity of resources among nations and the conflicts of interest between them. Yet the rapid changes and formidable challenges facing agricultural development demand not only coordination but innovation in promoting new ventures. If development institutions do not encourage changes and share the risk in making them, what is their purpose? Frank Meissner's recollection of some of the more innovative projects supported by the IDB demonstrates that a development institution can be a partner in changing old patterns and promoting new approaches to development. We hope these experiences inspire new avenues for progress in the future.

In Latin America and around the world, a generation has seen the specter of Malthus' law suspended, only to be replaced by a "food chain of affluence." Efficient and modern agricultural development will exile Malthus' law to history, in practice as well as in theory. The goal must be to establish an affordable food chain in which sustainable agriculture bolsters the economic development of consumers and farmers alike.

INTRODUCTION

BY NANCY MORRISON

Around the world, billions of people live with a paradox. They are hungry, sick and poor—yet experts already have the technical knowledge to solve those problems. Specialists in agriculture and nutrition have gained the ability to grow enough food to feed all the world's people. Medical experts know how to conquer many of the diseases that have cut life short for millennia. The knowledge exists to purify water, to pump and channel and store it: a riddle of life that stumped generations. Through trial-and-error, we're even learning the economic schemes that work best in different settings to unleash the energy and talent that produce prosperity.

What's missing is the *transfer* of skills, knowledge, resources, money, and willpower to make lives around the world healthier and wealthier. This book examines three decades of lessons about the economic, social and cultural distribution of these elements of development. It focuses on Latin America—Central and South America and the Caribbean.

The lessons are sweeping, yet often simple. The people who live with development strategies must be actively involved in the planning and executing of those strategies. Those who are left out will have little incentive to continue with development activities once development experts and officials pack up and leave.

On the U.S.-Mexican border, that lesson is evident. In the early 1960s, as massive investments in irrigation were being launched in western Mexico, some Mexican farmers foresaw that the best future for their irrigated land lay in raising high-quality fruits and vegetables for export to the vast U.S. and Canadian markets. They established a national union to link Mexican growers with U.S. distributors. In time, the distribution system became a truly bi-national industry, as U.S. and Mexican companies worked together to market farm commodities. The empowerment of Mexican farmers became a major—if little known—achievement of a huge investment in irrigation, one that came from the people themselves (see pp. 70-72).

As those Mexican farmers showed, some of the best ideas for development projects come not from outside "experts", but from the people those projects aim to help. That lesson was seen again among some small merchants—mainly women—in San Salvador. The women, most of them vendors with small market stalls, needed to borrow funds to buy their wares from wholesalers. But the only money-lenders they could turn to charged sky-high interest rates. The women banded together to form a mutual savings-and-credit association. The group approached commercial banks for revolving lines-of-credit for working capital and soon obtained loans at a fraction of the interest rate they had been paying. The Salvadoran merchants didn't stop there. They organized daycare for their children, arranged for low-cost food for pregnant women, and lined up legal, technical, and credit assistance for members. Their self-help efforts became a model for loans to help set up markets offered by one development institution, the Inter-American Development Bank (see pp. 35-37). The challenge for such institutions is to be smart enough to notice and endorse good local ideas and flexible enough to help make them work. A flexible loan repayment system helped cash-strapped Argentine farmers launch new enterprises and cope with raging inflation. The key was to let farmers repay farm loans in their crop—honey—rather than cash. The success of the program helped create jobs and slow the exodus of the area's young people to cities (see pp. 33-35).

Some lessons that emerge from the book are more complex. Balancing environmental protection and economic development involves difficult trade-offs, which are only now beginning to be understood. High in the Ecuadoran Andes, ways to protect the fragile environment are being explored. The poor Indians who live in the area have an urgent need for wood as fuel and as a cash crop. Plantations now being established promise a long-term wood supply. As the trees grow, the Indians can gather firewood from thinning and fallen branches. In time, their children will have mature trees to harvest (see pp. 100-101).

One lesson permeates the book. Development is a constant process of attuning, of trial and error. New technologies are tested. New management techniques are tried. New bonds are formed, as when farmers band together to irrigate their fields or women unite to sell their crafts. Sometimes, old bonds are strained and shatter.

The stories in this book describe that process. They trace the sometimes smooth, sometimes faltering patterns of development in projects throughout Latin America. Some of these projects have withstood the test of time. Others have not. Still others were sidetracked—by war, or debt, or lack of skills or understanding.

Taken together, these stories reveal ways to consolidate the gains of the past and avoid mistakes in the future. At their best, they promise improvements that can, quite simply, make life better for millions of the world's poor.

The book focuses on the experience of one institution, the Inter-American Development Bank (IDB). Since its start in 1959, the Bank has become a major catalyst in mobilizing resources for Latin America's development. It has helped marshal financing for projects that, in all, total more than $136 billion. The IDB also works to distribute the benefits of development more equitably, particularly by backing projects to improve the lives of lower-income Latin Americans.

The book is the extraordinary testament of an experienced and sensitive development official, Frank Meissner. In 18 years of work on development projects in Latin America for the IDB, Dr. Meissner recorded a series of successes and failures. This book is the result of his conscientiousness in pondering those episodes.

For Dr. Meissner, every development endeavor was an experiment and thus an opportunity to learn. His perspective was that of a scientist: each experiment was a success because it added to the store of knowledge. The success or failure of a particular plan or project was less important than the fact that an effort was made and a new idea or approach was tried—thus enlarging the base upon which to build and improve subsequent development activities. Each effort could yield data or insights that could lead to other initiatives. The steady accumulation of effort would produce an overall system that could improve the lives of millions. The challenge, Dr. Meissner energetically insisted, is to learn from the past—and to press forward with the best lessons, without losing momentum and without becoming defeatist.

Dr. Meissner focused his energy and optimism on some of life's most basic enterprises—farming, fishing, and forestry. But his focus was not simply on resource production. Rather, the book he left behind takes a comprehensive view: one that, for instance, looks at agricultural development from the time a new high-yielding variety of seed is developed in a laboratory until the time food grown from those seeds is sold on supermarket shelves and farmers begin to reap the financial rewards.

Along the way, the book examines research, financing, marketing, environmental protection, livestock production, irrigation, land settlement, and rural poverty—the range of activities that branch out from farming, fishing, and forestry and upon which final success rests.

The book's ultimate focus is on people's lives, especially the social organizations that evolve as they farm, fish, and live and work in forests. To make their work more productive, people often forge communities of interest that allocate responsibilities and benefits. Thus, farmers form cooperatives to share the costs of irrigation and market their crops. Merchants band together to pool their savings and tap commercial credit. This is a human book and its most enduring themes emerge through stories with the common touch. In these vignettes, readers will meet and hear the voices of people whose lives are affected by development activities.

The stories are not always neat. Not all move forward in one dramatic line and snap closed with a resounding ending like good drama. Real life is messier than fiction, and in some of these stories, war, inflation, or lack of understanding intervene to postpone the ending. Not all those endings are happy. But all the stories present important insights, and the book aims to pass them on to those who can build upon them.

Each chapter begins with an introduction that sets the social and economic scene for a broad topic, such as marketing or fisheries. The vignettes follow. From these, several themes emerge.

The first step of a development initiative—for instance, granting land titles to families who for generations have been landless—is often the most dynamic element of change. This is a lesson from life: the movement from nothing to something is a greater leap than the movement from sufficiency to abundance.

Research is a key to great gains. Through research, innovations are discovered, and through demonstrations and other extension services, innovations spread. Research and extension have brought development institutions such as the IDB some of the biggest rewards for their development dollars by making agriculture, fisheries, and forestry more productive and profitable throughout the developing world.

Markets are another pivotal means of distribution. The unfettered exchange of goods and services can liberate energy and creativity. Isolated women in rural Uruguay demonstrate the value of markets. A group of ranchers' wives took a traditional skill , knitting, formed a crafts cooperative, and fashioned sophisticated sweaters and knitwear that today sell around the world. Thanks to their earnings, their families and their communities are far more comfortable. The social changes the women fostered in rural Uruguay were as great as the economic. "The men scoffed at first," recalled one of them. "They called us the 'crazy old wool women.' Now everyone is very respectful. They call us the 'money women'" (see pp. 20-24).

Empowerment is a major theme of the book and is particularly important in Latin America for women, the backbone of the rural economy. In El Salvador, in a region long plagued by poverty, a cooperative of local women is sharing a recipe for economic success. They launched a food processing plant using their own initiative, resources easily available to their community, foreign expertise, and partnerships with two international groups: the Overseas Education Fund and the IDB. Their efforts are lifting an entire region out of poverty and cutting their nation's dependence on imports (see pp. 6-9).

Empowerment is also crucial for rural communities, such as the small Andean town of Laguna Azul in Colombia. There, even a modest market access road means more than transport. The road connects the community to the nation's economic mainstream and paves the way to development. An IDB-backed road building program near Laguna Azul provided another benefit: it created a new group of local construction entrepreneurs. Using the most simple tools—picks and shovels—local farmers and workers opened their community and earned self-esteem (see pp. 10-12).

Another theme that runs through the book is the proven value of innovation. These projects encourage imagination, risk-taking, and creativity, as the farmers in Peru's Ica Valley showed. For as long as local farmers could remember, cotton had been king in that irrigated region. But in the early 1980s, for the first time in the valley or Peru, farmers grew asparagus for export to North American markets. The switch was aided by an IDB-backed farm credit program, along with technical support through farmers' cooperatives. Now, grapes, mangoes, avocados, tomatoes and corn dot the valley (see pp. 37-40).

As innovations spread, they foster a flexible process of thinking, acting, and sharing that helps developing countries and development experts adapt to change. Such flexibility is needed if development is to be transformed from a series of individual projects to a long-term process of growth. Successfully transplanting that process could help the lives of millions.

Yet another theme unites the stories. The Inter-American Development Bank, a development institution, is itself developing. It has made mistakes and learned from them. It has broadened the range of services it offers Latin America. And it has expanded the scale and complexity of the development tasks it undertakes.

The Bank is moving through the 1990s with a challenge. The 1980s were a time of deprivation and disappointment for much of Latin America. The Bank must address the region's pent-up hopes. Imagination, creativity, and flexibility are needed as never before.

In meeting that challenge, IDB can build on 30 years of initiatives. Precedents exist in virtually every major area where the Bank must concentrate. But the challenges are great. One of the biggest is Latin America's high and growing rate of urbanization. The region is the only developing area where urbanization already matches the level of industrialized countries. By 1990, the region already had some of the world's biggest metropolitan areas. By the turn of the century, more than three-quarters of Latin America's population will live in cities.

Creativity is needed to meet the challenge. A supermarket chain in Chile provides a small but inspiring example. It used its profits, high volume sales, and know-how to supply low-cost food to the growing mass of urban consumers in Santiago. Profits generated in efficient supermarkets in middle- and high-income areas subsidized small mobile outlets that served consumers in Santiago's slums (see pp. 12-14).

Speeding the flight to Latin America's cities is the deterioration of rural life. Young people, in particular, need better prospects. Throughout Latin America, youth clubs modeled after U.S. 4-H Clubs are helping to slow the exodus to the cities by adding purpose and hope to young rural lives. Those clubs help young men and women gain valuable expertise in and around the farm and participate in community affairs (see pp. 51-53).

Among the region's most stubborn problems is land reform. Millions of Latin American farmers and their families are caught in a bind. They cannot get loans to operate or improve their farms, because most banks require collateral—and farmers do not own land that could serve as collateral. A simple innovation in farm credit is changing that. Under IDB-backed rural development schemes, thousands of farmers are buying title to their land from their governments. With those titles in hand, farmers can obtain loans through IDB-backed farm credit programs (see pp. 75-77).

Perhaps Latin America's most pressing economic problem is debt, which burdens both governments and businesses. One way to help companies reduce their debt is through equity investments. The power of that approach is demonstrated by a producer and distributor of veterinary products and insecticides in Ecuador. "Equity financing brought CAMPOSA more than just monetary benefits," said one of the firm's founders. "Before, we had a small company that operated in a small way." But working with IDB and a Dutch agency, CAMPOSA developed new kinds of information about finances and markets. And it learned how to launch new products (see pp. 42-44).

The will to change for the better, when coupled with the creative and intelligent distribution of skills, know-how, resources, and money, can make all the difference in development activities. That is the solution to the paradox of distribution and that is this book's message.

IDB AGRICULTURE, FISHERIES, AND FORESTRY PROJECTS — 1961-1990

Subsector	Number of Projects	Millions of U.S. Dollars	% of Total U.S. Dollars
Agricultural Credit	152	3,967.5	40.3
Irrigation and Drainage	91	2,109.5	21.5
Integrated Rural Development	38	1,032.0	10.5
Research and Extension	25	509.0	5.2
Fisheries and Aquaculture	35	472.0	4.8
Marketing Agro-industries	25	455.0	4.6
Livestock Development	24	346.0	3.5
Colonization and Settlement	23	299.0	3.0
Animal Health	18	166.0	1.7
Forestry	24	151.0	1.5
Other*	10	338.0	3.4
Total Agriculture/ Fisheries/Forestry	465	9,845.0	100.0

* Includes loans for $50 million approved in 1990 to Colombia for a program that covers sanitation, irrigation and management of swamps, land reclamation and forestation, and environmental management of the upper portion of the Bogotá River.

The creative power of entrepreneurship is recognized today, as never before, as a driving force that motivates people. It not only creates wealth, but liberates energy and creativity as well. Entrepreneurs are invigorating the Latin American economy, spreading their independent, creative spirit to the region's farms, forests, and fisheries. To turn ideas and energy into products and profits, entrepreneurs need basic investments. Roads must be built to bring products to market. Marketplaces are needed to sell the wares. A non-traditional approach to marketing—cooperatives—multiplies the energy and talents of entrepreneurs by enabling them to band together.

Such basic investments are only one link in the entrepreneurial lifeline. Imagination removes bottlenecks. Flexibility helps entrepreneurs avoid past mistakes and expand on past successes. The power of the entrepreneurial spirit, complemented by basic investments, is revealed in the following sections.

·

I

ENTREPRENEURSHIP

MARKETING

SMALL PROJECTS

MARKETING

Few things are more basic to life than adequate and reliable food supplies. At the center of the modern distribution of food lies the push and pull of the marketplace, which transforms the raw agricultural commodities produced by farmers into the foods bought and eaten by consumers. A poor understanding of these forces—and the resulting under-development of markets—will hamper the distribution of food in Latin America. The result will be shortages, malnutrition, and hunger: the paradox of hunger amidst plenty. Black markets, long waits for food, and crops rotting for lack of silos signal inadequate marketing systems.

Tackling the marketing of food means tackling a range of activities. At its most basic level, developing a market means actually constructing marketplaces—stalls, open air markets, and shops. Roads can be built to provide farmers with access to such marketplaces. Storage and food processing facilities can be established.

On a broader level, links between these local markets can evolve into regional, national, and international markets. For example, through high value-added activities such as growing and exporting specialty crops, producers in even remote corners of Latin America can find customers abroad.

Marketing embraces a wide range of policies and economic activities. Prices must evolve for products. Customers must be developed through advertising, promotion, and tailoring products to customers' needs and tastes. Credit needs to be extended to help farmers and shopkeepers finance their operations.

In Latin America, all these marketing activities require strengthening. Yet one marketing goal supersedes all others, from the viewpoint of development: bringing higher quality foodstuffs within the reach of poorer people. In much of the region, the food system is geared not to the needs of millions of poorer Latin Americans, but to a handful of affluent consumers at home and high-income customers abroad. A notable example is meat production, which traditionally has been based on feeding relatively cheap grain to animals to produce relatively expensive meat. In the process, more than half the calories and protein of the grains are lost. Meanwhile, inadequate nutrition—especially caloric intake and protein—is one of the most pressing problems facing the urban and rural poor.

To improve diets in Latin America, reorienting the market toward the broad base of consumers is key. This is especially important because the Latin population is increasingly urban and thus distant from rural sources of food. Nearly half the cost of food sold in cities comes not from the food itself, but from processing and distribution. More efficient marketing would cut costs, improve supplies, reduce delays for consumers, and boost producers' profits by boosting their total sales.

Moreover, marketing can lead to empowerment. Latin American farmers—the bulk of whom produce on small, scattered farms—gain power as they connect with regional, national, and even international markets. An effective marketing system also can distribute benefits more equitably among farmers, distributors, merchants, consumers, and government. For instance, if farmers have efficient and accurate prices to guide their decisions, they can know in advance where and when to take their products to market. Meanwhile, consumers, with the same information, can take advantage of price decreases.

In addition to aiding economic growth and nutritional well-being, good marketing practices can help promote national self-sufficiency in food—a significant advantage for countries with heavy loads of foreign debt.

The IDB's Role. To improve marketing, the IDB has focused on several key areas:

• **Grain storage, processing and marketing.** The IDB helped construct more than 400,000 tons of grain storage capacity in Latin America. The investments help distribute such mainstays of Latin American agriculture as grains, beans, and oil-bearing crops. These make up a large part of popular diets, are a prime source of income for small farmers, and generate substantial foreign exchange in Argentina, Brazil, Paraguay, Uruguay, and other countries.

• **Marketing facilities.** The IDB has helped build more than 1.5 million square feet of rural and urban public markets. In addition, IDB loans often support the assembly of foodstuffs in the countryside, as well as the shipping, retailing, and wholesaling of food products. The IDB's investments in city markets have helped improve the rising trade in food and fiber in the region's rapidly growing cities.

• **Agro-industrial projects.** Agro-industries produce, process, and distribute food. The IDB has funded more than 650 agro-industries, directly or indirectly. IDB loans have helped provide credit to raise crops and livestock; construct facilities to harvest, transport, process and package food; provide basic infrastructure, such as water, sewage, electricity, and communications systems; and supply equipment, machinery, and vehicles.

• **Technical assistance.** The IDB often helps strengthen borrowers' capacity to carry out projects related to marketing. For instance, the IDB helps hire experts to implement projects, provides scholarships to local technicians to study abroad, and backs vocational training. The IDB also helps improve public markets by backing steps to improve market information, advance product packaging and standards, conduct policy-oriented market research, and offer marketing education, training, and extension to producers and intermediaries.

• **Working capital.** The IDB has made funds for working capital an integral part of virtually all its global agricultural loans. Such loans help wholesalers and retailers purchase goods for resale and help producers buy such items as fuel, seeds, fertilizers and pesticides for their operations. The IDB-backed loans help borrowers avoid the high interest rates commonly charged by informal lenders. Because they "pay" less for their loans, borrowers need not pass on extra costs to consumers in the form of higher food prices.

In addition to its investments in marketing and agro-industries (see table on page xix), the IDB increasingly addresses marketing issues through other loans, including those backing credit, integrated rural development, livestock, forestry, fisheries, and aquaculture.

NEW PRODUCTS AND NEW LIVELIHOODS IN EL SALVADOR

In a region long plagued by poverty and unemployment, a cooperative of local women is sharing a recipe for economic success. They launched a food processing plant using their own initiative, resources easily available to their community, foreign expertise, and partnerships with two international groups: the Overseas Education Fund (OEF) and the IDB. Their efforts are lifting an entire region out of poverty and cutting their nation's dependence on imports.

Progress did not come easily. In the early 1970s, few economic opportunities existed in their village of El Castaño in western El Salvador, about 50 miles west of the capital city of San Salvador. Many villagers worked as domestics or grew food and raised animals to sell in local markets. Some migrated regularly to central El Salvador with their families to harvest coffee or cotton. They worked hard, yet they remained poor.

A club of housewives began a gardening project and started looking for ways to make money and improve the community's situation. They soon realized that they could accomplish in numbers what they could not do alone. The women worked first with a Salvadoran organization, the *Comité Pro Clubes de Amas de Casa Campesinas*, and then with the Overseas Education Fund (OEF), a nongovernment organization founded by the League of Women Voters that empowers peasant women to become small entrepreneurs. The OEF learned that although villagers lacked potable water and electricity, they grew tomatoes and fruits for home consumption. Yet, an OEF market survey showed that El Salvador imported virtually all its tomatoes and tomato products, mainly from Guatemala and other Central America neighbors. El Salvador's imports were soaring as its population grew.

Local production of fruits and vegetables as cash crops was discouraged by primitive marketing facilities, even though El Salvador had well-established means to produce and market traditional export products, such as coffee, sugar, and meat.

The OEF worked with the local women to set up a project to boost El Castaño's tomato production. With assistance from the United States Agency for International Development, the OEF arranged for special technical assistance to set up demonstration plots to help the community learn and test new production technology. New seed varieties and growing methods were introduced. These doubled yields. Once steady production was ensured, a community cooperative was formed in 1980, using as its base the original housewives' club. Eighty percent of the 160 members were women. Each member paid annual dues of two dollars and was taught the food processing and business skills needed to run the cooperative. With OEF's assistance, members obtained water and electricity for their community. Because only one-third of the co-op members had completed elementary school, OEF staff complemented its work with special courses in literacy, as

"El Castaño represents a people-to-people approach to economic assistance that is in the best tradition of the United States' concerns for its neighbors. Assistance such as that given to the El Castaño project ripples through two governments, one international bank, one small national economy,and one even smaller Central American community. It is the picture of what the most effective American aid to Central America can become."

— U.S. Senator Nancy L. Kassebaum
(Republican - Kansas)[1]

well as family health, nutrition, and child development. These improvements helped women earn regular and higher incomes. Today, they are feeding themselves and their families. They and their children are healthier.

The IDB advanced the project in 1983 when it provided a low-interest loan of $115,000 to El Castaño members to help them learn how to process tomatoes. Such concessional loans—characterized by

---

[1] Speech given at OEF's Annual Dinner, June 6, 1983.

interest rates ranging (in 1990) from one to four percent, extended grace periods ranging from five to ten years, and long-term amortization periods—represent nearly a quarter of the IDB's total lending, providing needed support for projects in the lesser developed Latin American countries.

In the case of El Castaño, the Bank expressed initial concern about the cooperative members' lack of experience with such a large-scale venture. A proposal to build a processing plant was put on hold. Instead, the cooperative launched a pilot project at an existing plant of the National Agricultural School. El Castaño and the Bank agreed that if the pilot operation proved successful, the IDB would consider backing a new vegetable processing plant near Sonsonate, close to El Castaño members and potential suppliers of raw materials.

By 1985, it was clear that the El Castaño project was ready to expand. The IDB extended $385,000 to fund a new canning plant, equipment, and initial operations of the new facility. Original equipment costs of $260,000 were cut in half when a technical expert found a metalworks shop in San Salvador to manufacture machinery. That move not only supported the national metal industry, but sliced costs for replacement parts.

The new plant employed 200 workers and helped another 2,400 people in 400 families, as new farmers and workers produced for the plant. Capacity jumped to 1,152 tons per year. By 1988, the plant was processing 1,700 tons of tomatoes a year and producing a range of products including tomato sauce and paste. Production from El Castaño successfully replaced all the catsup and canned tomatoes previously imported from Guatemala.

El Castaño also buys and raises a variety of fruits and vegetables in addition to tomatoes, including pineapples and jalapeño peppers. Commodities that are not sold fresh are processed into such products as catsup, sauces, and jam. Because most men work outside the village, selling their labor to farms in other areas, or farm their own land, women work in rotating shifts at the plant for daily wages. Instead of dividing profits among themselves, members re-invest their earnings to buy land farmed by community members who do not own property. By buying produce locally, the cooperative assures area farmers of stable markets at fair prices.

By 1990, El Castaño had grown from a group of 30 housewives looking for a way to make money to a profitable business that has improved the lives of more than 6,000 local women and their families. El Castaño's progress has spread throughout the region. Co-op members are lending their special expertise in small business development to surrounding communities. The food-processing plant brought electricity to the area. Once the main electrical lines were installed for the factory, it was not long before every village in the area was electrified.

Two co-op members illustrate the changes that have come to El Castaño—especially its women. In 1980, Natividad Pérez was a poor, illiterate woman living in a peaceful region of troubled El Salvador. At age 36, she had begun to learn to read and write, but lacked motivation to pursue her studies.

Then, in 1981, a close friend invited Natividad to join the El Castaño Cooperative, then two years old. She soon supervised a production line at the processing plant. As supervisor, she needed to read and write to process paperwork. With this added incentive, she became literate. She even carries her work home. In the evenings, Natividad and her teenage son experiment in their home kitchen to develop new products.

Another co-op member, María Antonia Pérez, comes from a peasant farming family in El Castaño. When she was 19, María Antonia began to work part-time at El Castaño, helping with administration. When she completed high school, she went on to get an advanced degree in business administration. Unlike many of El Salvador's educated young people, María Antonia did not leave the countryside to seek a job in the city. Instead, she stayed in El Castaño and was chosen by the members to manage the co-op.

In short, El Castaño is more than a commercial success. It has become a symbol of the achievements of rural women and a centerpiece for a series of development projects that are raising the regional standard of living.

CONNECTING MARKETS IN COLOMBIA

Even a modest dirt or gravel road can be the difference between isolation and economic opportunity for a small Andean town such as Laguna Azul. A road connects the community to the nation's economic mainstream by helping farmers get their produce to market and bring supplies home. An IDB-backed road building program near Laguna Azul provided another benefit: it created a new group of local entrepreneurs.

The road-building program gave local farmers and workers a chance to become construction entrepreneurs using the most simple tools: picks and shovels. Largely because of this "primitive" technology—not despite it— the program has been a great success.

The project began in 1980, when the U.S. Agency for International Development helped fund an experimental road-building effort. Colombia's National Fund for Rural Roads then launched a national program to build about 500 kilometers of roads in 75 sections of 8 to 12 kilometers each. The IDB contributed more than half the program's overall cost of $33 million.

Pick-and-shovel technology was chosen because in a hilly region often above cloud level, road construction can be difficult and dangerous. Heavy machinery cannot be used because it can cause accidents and damage small land parcels. The most efficient method is to combine picks-and-shovels with small-scale soil-moving and compacting equipment.

Picapaleros, the local workers using picks and shovels (*pico y pala*), worked not as laborers, but as small-scale entrepreneurs. Local farmers or workers were contracted to complete individual "tasks," each equalling about 20 meters of road. Each task took about 20 to 30 days to finish, depending on amount of earth and rock to be moved, the *picapalero's* efficiency, and the size of the crew. *Picapaleros* were paid when the work was done. Most efficient entrepreneurs completed two or more tasks.

The pick-and-shovel roads slashed the costs of getting goods to market. José Humberto Bejarano, who makes cheese for sale in Bogotá, explained, "A trip [to a transport point] that used to take five hours on foot now takes less than one hour by truck. The 25 kilograms of cheese I send weekly to the market now arrive on time and in good condition. With the extra income, I was able to buy bicycles for my children to use on the new road."

The road has benefitted the village of Laguna Azul, as well. The new roads replace ancient mule paths and can be used by trucks and buses. Before the route was built, vegetables sold in the village had to be shipped from Bogotá, some 250 kilometers away. Now produce comes directly from surrounding farms. Enrollment at the community school has risen as children in outlying areas travel by bus. Commerce has increased.

In the 1980s, labor-intensive pick-and-shovel technology—based on local entrepreneurship, tools, and raw materials—gradually became a standard means of building and maintaining rural roads in regions throughout Latin America where labor is abundant and its use cost effective.

In 1983, the IDB backed the Guatemalan Bureau of Highways' efforts to conduct a rural roads study. One result was a manual that outlined methods of labor-intensive road construction that could be used for a variety of projects. Later, the IDB lent Guatemala funds to build or improve 400 kilometers of rural roads in the nation's central highlands. The new route replaced a track that clogged with mud when it rained, preventing farmers from shipping out their crops. Much of the road work was done by *picapaleros,* such as a 14-kilometer stretch near Tecpán that employed 200 people for more than a year.

Picks and shovels also are flying in Honduras, where 80 percent of the work on a project to build 173 kilometers of new rural access roads has been labor-intensive, bringing jobs to areas with high rates of unemployment. Construction of the rural roads is part of a nationwide program begun in 1986 to improve roads throughout Honduras, backed by IDB loans totaling $29 million.

In Bolivia, an Emergency Social Fund designed to ease the effect of economic adjustment policies on the poor has financed several labor-intensive road and civil works projects to create employment. IDB funds have supported these efforts.

The *picapalero* method has strengthened the skills of communities to move themselves forward, propelling rural small-scale entrepreneurship. The projects not only link rural areas to marketing centers and generate employment, but also demonstrate to workers that "they can do it."

SUPERMARKETS IN CHILE

One of the most pressing problems facing Latin American cities is how to supply low-cost food to the growing mass of urban consumers. Cities in Latin America began to grow rapidly in the late 1950s. More time and effort was needed to get food from farms to the increasing numbers of city-dwellers. Marketing costs soared, and with them, the price of food. The urban poor were especially hurt; primitive marketing in low-income districts caused the poor to pay 20-30 percent more for their food than the people in wealthier areas, where trade was better organized and more competitive.

Middle- and high-income areas were often the first to attract supermarkets in Latin America, even such cooperatives as the Hogar Obrero supermarkets in Argentina. How could a development institution such as the IDB help bring the benefits of mass-marketing consumer staples to the urban poor?

An opportunity arose in the early 1960s, shortly after the IDB began its operations. In 1961, a small, private consumer cooperative (UNICOOP) was launched in Santiago, Chile to buy food, clothing, and household and personal items for wholesale or retail distribution.

By 1962, UNICOOP had two supermarkets in Santiago. In 1963,

UNICOOP asked the IDB for a $600,000 loan to pay half the costs of building four more supermarkets in low- and middle-income neighborhoods and a central distribution warehouse.

UNICOOP began to buy fresh produce directly from farmers, bypassing traditional wholesale markets. By cutting out the middleman, UNICOOP could pay farmers 15 to 30 percent more than they had received in the colorful old Vega Central wholesale market. Moreover, UNICOOP could sell fresh produce of better quality in its retail outlets at prices 5 to 10 percent below those of competitors. UNICOOP charged the same retail prices in all outlets, in spite of higher cost and no real competition in the poorer districts. It expressly used some profits generated in the efficient supermarkets of the wealthier districts to subsidize the stores in low-income areas that did not pay for themselves.

UNICOOP soon came to be the largest grocery-buyer in Chile and could command substantial discounts on merchandise. Operations succeeded so well that in 1969, the IDB lent another $2.5 million to build eight more supermarkets and expand the central warehouse. To help Santiago slum-dwellers better benefit from the chain's "economies of scale," the IDB devised an unprecedented loan structure. IDB funds were used exclusively to build supermarkets in low-income areas, while private investors financed stores in wealthier areas. In addition, a concessionary special fund was set aside to launch a system of mobile markets to serve consumers in Santiago's slums one fixed day each week.

By 1972, eight mobile markets were in action. UNICOOP also operated 18 supermarkets, eight of them in low-income areas. More than 100,000 people belonged to the co-op. Sales topped $36 million.

UNICOOP soon became the prototype of a "socially conscious" commercial marketing system. Owing much of its success to excellent management, the cooperative hired, trained and maintained a dedicated staff throughout its wide-ranging operations. It actively involved many members in a wide variety of commercial and social activities. Members were eligible for special monthly refunds. Life insurance programs were offered. During 1972-1973, when food was sometimes scarce in Chile, the cooperative provided its members with packets of food essentials.

By the mid-1970s, however, the economic and political climate of Chile had changed. Government policies made the cooperative savings system practically inoperable, and UNICOOP was forced to sell out to private investors in 1976. The investors who acquired UNICOOP changed the name to UNIMARC S.A. and MULTIAHORRO S.A. Both private companies successfully expanded in medium- and high-income areas and branched out to Chile's provinces. Twenty-five of the supermarkets are still in operation today—but the unique social purpose of the cooperative effectively ended with UNICOOP.

Despite this ambiguous ending, UNICOOP's early innovations and successes showed that the cooperative supermarket system could be adapted to other Latin American countries. Through UNICOOP, it was demonstrated that mass marketing can help bring reasonably-priced food to low-income urban families and help distribute the benefits of marketing improvements more equitably among producers and consumers by working directly with agro-industries and farmers.

MARKETING RICE IN ECUADOR

The fertile region where the Babahoyo, Daule, and Guayas Rivers empty into the Pacific is justly called the breadbasket of Ecuador. Along these coastal lowlands north of the port city of Guayaquil, farmers produce 90 percent of the country's rice and half of its bananas, as well as coffee, cacao, and other agricultural products.

While the land is rich, most of the people who live in the Daule region have long been poor. Their fortunes did not improve even after large farms were broken up under agrarian reforms in the 1960s. Small farmers continued to be beholden to large rice mills. They needed credit to plant crops, but commercial banks did not consider them creditworthy. Mill-owners lent working capital at no interest. But at harvest time, they demanded farmers' crops—at prices and conditions set by owners. Farmers remained trapped in a web of dependency.

Breaking out of this web became the task for Ecuador's National Federation of Agricultural and Marketing Cooperatives. The Federation is made up of 49 associated cooperatives in nine of Ecuador's provinces. Among these are 15 associated rice cooperatives embracing

500 low-income families in the area of Daule. The Federation clearly understood the basic problem troubling the small farmer. "The crop he planted was never his," explained Jorge Salvador López, the Federation's General Manager. "It belonged to someone else the minute he put the seed in the ground."

Even those unfavorable credit arrangements with mill operators were better than other options. Farm supply stores charged excessively steep interest rates on loans. And the state development bank took too much time approving or granting credit.

The Federation decided to buy rice from its members at a fair market price and mill the crop in the area. With the help of a $400,000 grant from the Inter-American Foundation, the Federation bought vehicles and equipment and obtained working capital to carry out its plan. The Federation also joined the Central Farmers Market in Quito, which was built with IDB funds. The Federation distributed half the profits from rice sales in the Central Market to members. It kept the other half to provide working capital to finance the next rice crop.

For two years, the new system worked according to plan. Then, mill operators began to retaliate. "They realized that we were becoming serious competition," Señor López explained. "So they tried to get us out of the way by closing their doors and refusing to mill our rice."

In response, the Federation rented an old mill. This provided valuable operating experience in milling and demonstrated that farmers had growing economic clout. Within a year, the Federation decided to build and equip its own rice milling and drying plant. But they lacked funds for the considerable investment.

A chance encounter with an IDB staffer dramatically changed the Federation's fortunes. At a seminar sponsored by Ecuador's Bank for Cooperatives, Carlos Cassacia, an IDB small project specialist, met Señor López, who proceeded to explain why the Federation needed its own rice mill. Cassacia grasped the project's potential. He helped plan the project and shepherded the loan request through the Bank. Funds were approved in 1983.

By the IDB's standards, the loan was not large: $500,000 from the Small Projects Program, through a special fund established by the Swiss government. Some $325,000 was earmarked for construction; the remainder was set aside for working capital to buy rice for the mill.

In all, the project totalled $1.5 million. The plant was built using equipment made in Brazil. The Bank tapped the Swiss fund to finance administrative training for Federation personnel. The plant was inaugurated in June, 1985. All of the Federation's rice-producing cooperatives in the Daule area participated in the venture. Each farmer paid about $10 as an initiation fee and bought six investment certificates of about $10 each to provide the Federation with working capital and promotion. The new mill helped break the web of dependence. "Before, I lived in a shack in the country," said one cooperative member who farms three hectares. "Now I live in town, and I have moved into a better house."

The project transformed Daule's small-scale rice farmers into independent producers, free to negotiate the sale of their product and enjoy the financial rewards they deserve from their labors.

SMALL PROJECTS, BIG RESULTS

When traffic slows in Costa Rica, vendors dart out to waiting cars to sell fried plantains. In Peru, moviegoers avoid long waits in ticket lines by buying their tickers not from movie houses, but from entrepreneurs who buy stacks of tickets hours before the show starts. In cities throughout Latin America, the cab drivers racing through city traffic may be moonlighting doctors or mechanics.

On the streets and in homes throughout Latin America, a vital, endlessly innovative type of economic activity is flourishing: the so-called informal sector—small businesses not registered with the government. These enterprises make up an astonishing 30 to 40 percent of the region's economy and contain some of its most energetic and imaginative business men and women. IDB Senior Policy Officer Luis Ratinoff calls them "the last true entrepreneurs, willing to risk everything, and not get caught up in the bureaucratic in-fighting of the corporate world."

Often these entrepreneurs must operate without enough space, training, or equipment. Steps are being taken to tap this vital energy.

The Other Path. It was Hernando de Soto, through his book, *The Other*

Path: The Informal Revolution (El Otro Sendero: La Revolución Informal), who focused widespread attention on the informal sector. In a book that later became a best-seller in Latin America, de Soto, director of Lima's Institute for Liberty and Democracy (ILD), asked a question startling in its simplicity. Why, after a century of industrialization, massive infusions of capital, technological improvements, and hard work, and why, after decades of development following World War II, has much of Latin America remained hobbled by low economic growth and riddled with poverty? De Soto's conclusion was clear: something was seriously amiss with the conventional wisdom—not only of development specialists, but their critics on the political left and right, as well.

De Soto set out to find some answers to his questions in Peru. There, he began to formulate a strategy for development that built upon a realistic understanding of the ingredients of prosperity. He relied on strict empirical observation of how and why incomes are actually made and spent.

The ILD approach rested on two conclusions. First, the entrepreneurial element of the economy—an element that is key to employment, capital formation, and growth—is squeezed by governments throughout Latin America. Second, development professionals have not fully grasped the fundamental link between economic participation and political empowerment in creating a modern prosperous economy.

ILD surveys found that in Latin America, nearly three-fifths of the urban population work in the gray economy. How, the ILD asked, can governments expect to maintain social and political stability when their economic authority extends to less than two-fifths of the population?

The ILD has begun to articulate a pragmatic policy agenda for Peru that reaches out to the informal sector. The ILD drafted legislation on property titles; organized an ombudsman system to oversee court proceedings; pushed through an initiative that greatly expanded access to banking credit by broadening the definition of collateral; made government policy statements available to the general public; and gathered signatures to endorse new laws. These changes aimed at insuring more open rule-making and more reasonable application of the law. Through its activism, the ILD showed that such steps can be politically attractive. If politicians can be shown that they will gain popularity for taking a public-minded course, they will so act.

The IDB's Role. Even before the ILD was spreading its message about actively involving the informal sector in government, the IDB was ready to take a chance on micro-entrepreneurship.

In 1978, a full decade before de Soto's book burst on the scene, the IDB devised a completely new means to reach out and help small entrepreneurs: the Small Projects Program (SPP). The SPP extends credit to low-income individuals and groups that lack credit experience, collateral, and resources and thus cannot obtain credit from conventional public and commercial sources.

Thanks to credit mobilized by the Bank, a whole new class of low-income borrowers can now expand productive rural and urban enterprises. Beneficiaries often see their incomes rise by as much as 300 percent and their security grow through the creation of jobs. Equally important is the confirmation that they are productive members of society, rather than permanently on or beyond the fringes.

Borrowers tap IDB-backed credit through public development agencies and non-profit intermediaries such as cooperatives, foundations, and producers' associations. To reach low-income people, IDB field offices help identify non-governmental organizations (NGOs)—including workers' associations, religious organizations, and labor groups. With the IDB's help, these groups can stretch limited resources to provide technical assistance and credit to poor borrowers.

Small project borrowers benefit from more liberal terms than conventional Bank financing: amortization periods are up to 40 years, typically with 10-year grace periods. The IDB does not collect a fee to cover its administrative costs and does not require that repayment terms be adjusted to compensate for the local currency's loss of purchasing power.

Governments also help. For example, in Guatemala, power from the National Electrification Institute was essential to a project to bring water from the Rio de los Platanos to 200 subsistence farms owned by members of the cooperative at San Miguel Conacaste, north of Guatemala City. An IDB loan and grant financed pumps, an aqueduct, storage tanks and irrigation distribution schemes installed to boost production of tomatoes, cucumbers, corn, and beans. Beneficiaries' per capita incomes ranged from $50 to $133.

"The whole community participated in that project, working to overcome the challenge of getting the water over a 1,000-meter hill," said Ken Cole, Coordinator of the Small Projects Program. Five years after approval of the financing, tomato production in the area was 60 percent higher than the national average and chili pepper output had risen six-fold. Some 114 new jobs had been created.

By 1991, the IDB had approved 222 small projects for a total of $88.7 million. The SPP had directly benefitted more than 120,000 low-income farmers, small-scale entrepreneurs, and artisans. Another 200,000 people have participated in SPP-related management and technical training. Although small in size, SPP projects have often spurred innovations and fostered the development of entrepreneurship in the informal sector throughout Latin America.

Women are major direct beneficiaries of Bank-backed small projects, in such areas as crafts, micro-enterprise, and agro-industry. Many women borrowers are also raising children and managing homes: their high degree of responsibility carries over to their micro-enterprises. The women generally have excellent repayment records, often qualify for increasing amounts of credit, and, according to various reviews of various projects, are able to increase family income and consolidate their enterprises.

With their livelihoods on the line, SPP borrowers have proven to be good credit risks. Late payments average 10 percent or less in most programs, and the default rate is below five percent—a figure that Bank officials say compares favorably with the banking sector in general.

More than half of IDB-backed small projects are in the agriculture sector, including financing for crops for small farmers, financing of livestock, agro-industry, youth clubs, irrigation and fishing. For example, a highway may cost hundreds of millions of dollars and link remote areas and major markets. But it does little to help farmers, livestock raisers, and artisans —they lack money to pay for raw materials and breeding stock, vehicles to transport their output to market, expertise in marketing their products, and credit to keep going in the off-season.

"It's not through the large infrastructure projects that you reach the poor directly," explained an IDB project evaluation officer. "We have to think of the trucks and the people in the trucks, as well as of the highway." IDB also targets micro-enterprises, very small businesses generally owned or operated by one person with 10 or fewer employees—often relatives. Market and street vendors, repairmen, shoe-shine boys—all operate in the informal sector, providing the goods and services that fuel the local economy and furnish important support for national and even international economies. About one-third of the IDB's SPP loans have gone to such micro-enterprises. The SPP has been such a huge success in its first decade that during the 1990s, the Bank plans to increase its support of micro-enterprises. The aim is to help these micro-enterprises overcome bottlenecks that affect their growth and prospects.

Such help is especially needed because of the growing demand for jobs in the region. In the 1990s, it is expected that upwards of 40 million people will be entering the workforce in Latin America, mainly in the cities. Self-employment in the informal sector is the only option for many. By 1995, the IDB aims to provide a mix of technical assistance, small project financing, global loans, guarantee funds, and pre-investment support for micro-producers in all Latin American borrowing countries.

CRAFTING A FUTURE IN URUGUAY

"The men scoffed at first. They called us the 'crazy old wool women.' Now everyone is very respectful. They call us 'the money women.'"

Rufina Román de Viera is talking about an enterprising crafts cooperative in Uruguay that fashions woven and handicraft items for export. With a big dose of entrepreneurship, the group has thrived—and so have rural lives.

The group is *Manos del Uruguay* (Hands of Uruguay) and its success is remarkable. Founded in 1968 by a small group of women in

Montevideo, the cooperative aimed to increase the incomes of rural women by helping its members produce and sell handwoven and knit articles. The cooperative eventually obtained the financial resources that helped it grow into a model for handicrafts enterprises around the world.

"Knitting was a tradition—we started with a saddle blanket, changed its color, gave it a face lift, and had a throw rug," explained Isabel Gallinal de Terra, who began working with *Manos* as a social worker and in time became the president of the organization. "At first, we made sweaters that were so heavy that they guaranteed instant curvature of the spine."

In such modest beginnings, the IDB saw the thread of creativity. In 1979, IDB put up $500,000 to help *Manos* buy wool and machinery, including spinning machines, looms, dyeing vats, thermometers, and driers. The Bank also supplied working capital, training, and marketing assistance. Such investments aimed at more than simply improving output. It also aimed to slow migration to cities, boost employment, and raise women's incomes.

Soon *Manos del Uruguay* sweaters became familiar sights in fashionable shops not only in Uruguay, but elsewhere in South America, the United States, Western Europe and Japan, as well. Over time, *Manos* has become one of the largest employers in Uruguay's rural areas. It has expanded to process cotton and silk garments, to complement its basic line of wool items, and offers ceramic, wood, and textile items for household decor.

Women entrepreneurs have especially prospered. The first round of financing helped *Manos* manage a network of 18 cooperative handicraft groups throughout Uruguay that grew to about 1,000 women members. The central service unit in Montevideo drew on a staff of nearly 100 to provide technical assistance, buy raw materials, and provide marketing services for the entire *Manos* system.

Under the IDB-backed project, 500 new crafts producers joined cooperatives. Manos' sales quadrupled to some $3.7 million from 1977 to 1983. During that time, exports jumped from half to three-quarters of total sales. The export success was all the greater considering that Uruguayan country-women, unlike women in the Andes, Mexico and Guatemala, had never knitted anything distinctive. "We have no indigenous tradition here," said Beatriz Gulla, who heads the design staff. "We had to create our own tradition."

By 1986, designs included burgundy-colored peacocks, stylized horse heads, purple butterflies flirting with orange tulips, black cats eerily stalking across skyscraper roofs, and designs inspired by abstract artists and primitive painters.

The social revolution that *Manos* created in rural Uruguay was as important as its economic impact. Rufina Román de Viera, a country woman in her late 40s who has served as one of *Manos'* managers, exemplifies the change. "I live on a farm and I had three years of schooling," she explained. "At 16, I got married, and soon had seven children. I never had a chance to do anything, except once I took a correspondence course in dressmaking. Ten years ago, I joined the *Manos* cooperative as an opportunity to better myself. But first I had to educate my husband. There were great debates the first few years about my leaving the house. We would run out of bread, or one of the kids would catch a cold—the little things that always happen. But it was worse for my husband because I was not at home. When I would come home late from a meeting, he would say, 'I want to know what's going on there. Why were you gone so long?'"

Crafts work is time-consuming and painstaking. Fashioning a sweater takes 10 to 40 hours, depending on the complexity of the design. The artisan gets 65 percent of the wholesale price and may net $100 a month—princely pay in the Uruguayan countryside. Jacinto, Rufina's husband, an itinerant farm mechanic, seldom earned that much. Neither did the ranch hands, policemen, soldiers, truck drivers and minor government officials who were the husbands of other rural artisans. Social workers tried to smooth the ruffled machismo of unlettered but proud men whose earnings were unexpectedly eclipsed by their wives.

But results won out over resistance. Now visitors from around the world flock to *Manos* to look, learn, and write about the program. From *Manos*, they can learn clear lessons about innovative ways to mobilize talent; enlist help from socially-conscious members of the establishment; imaginatively use networks of "connections" to expand local and export markets; effectively translate market demand into product development; and train workers to assume more managerial power.

The IDB helped launch handicraft projects in the image of *Manos* in many countries during the 1970s and 1980s. Variations on the theme occurred in:

Bolivia, where woolen garments have long served as means of keeping warm in the rugged highlands. Today, weaving has a new aim: to upgrade living standards for weavers and their communities. Artisans are increasingly making sweaters, ponchos, and other clothing through organized efforts. An SPP loan to a private non-profit Bolivian association has helped establish a self-sustaining community of 100 rural families, one-third of whom work in a handicrafts workshop and garment factory. They export most of their products to Europe.

Colombia. The first Colombian craftsmen worked in copper, bronze and gold, fashioning articles of great beauty. Today's artisans continue this tradition. Many craftsmen work with *Artesanías de Colombia*. This independent government institution, with the help of small-project financing from the IDB, has established revolving lines of credit to help craftsmen and women obtain working capital, as well as tools, kilns, looms and other basic materials. This will help provide access to credit for craftsmen who do not have access to other channels of conventional credit, while enabling them to diversity their production lines and expand their productivity.

Guatemala. The forms, colors and designs of Guatemalan handicrafts date back to the Mayan culture. An IDB-backed program provided design and production assistance to artisans and helped them adapt products for international markets. Now, contemporary handicrafts groups can get financial support from any of several small projects in the country.

While consumers may view such handicrafts as a link with the past, artisans see their product as a bridge to the future. Handicrafts sold in city boutiques can mean a better life back in the village. Helping artisans to capitalize on what they know has generated dramatic results. Handicrafts backed by IDB projects are now sold not only locally, but in prestigious shops in New York, Buenos Aires, Madrid, Rome, London, and Paris, as well.

Manos was a happy choice for the IDB's first Small Project. It not only demonstrated the viability of the concept, but served as a model for other artisan projects—so much so that Mariann Tadmor, the IDB's craft specialist, has become a recognized source of the state-of-the-art knowledge about starting, organizing and managing small craft enterprises in Latin American countries.

A NEW LOOK AT ANCIENT GRAINS IN PERU

The rich and varied native grains of Latin America were staple foods during the reigns of the Incas, Aztecs and other pre-Colombian peoples. But production and consumption of the grains declined throughout the colonial period along with the once-mighty Indian civilizations that cultivated them.

By the middle of this century in Peru, the ancient grains were in virtual productive extinction as cash crops, replaced by cheap wheat imports and shunned by increasingly urbanized populations. Cultivation was limited primarily to subsistence farmers in the barren High Sierra region, mostly poor Quechua-speaking families, many headed by women. With virtually no access to agricultural extension services and credit, the women and the families they supported were as much on the margin of the Andean economy as the forgotten grains they were producing.

Then, in the mid-1970s, interest in healthy and alternative food sources resurged in Peru and abroad. The high nutritional value of the native grains was rediscovered, with potential benefits not only for the impoverished grain farmers but for many malnourished Peruvians.

The native grains are suited to the difficult growing conditions of the Andean region. Kaniwa (*Chenopodium pallidicaule*) is 14 percent protein and contains essential amino acids that complement the vegetables often eaten in the area. Tarhui (*Lupinus mutabilis*), a pod-bearing plant resistant to cold, can also be grown in poor, high-altitude soils. A high alkaloid content makes it bitter and toxic; a simple water extraction process, developed by ancient Aztecs, renders it palatable. Quinoa (*Chenopodium quinoa*) can be grown under particularly unfavorable conditions at elevations of between 3,000 and 4,000 meters, on poorly drained lands. Referred to in the Quechua language as the "mother grain", quinoa was so important to the Incas that each year the Inca emperor broke the soil with a golden spade and planted the first seed. Quinoa can have as much as double the protein value of common cereal grains.[2]

Of special interest is amaranth, a fine-seeded, ragged-looking cousin of red-root pigweed; it may have been cultivated in some parts of the world for as long as 5,000 years and was once almost as broadly cultivated throughout the Americas as corn.[3] Spanish soldiers who

[2] National Research Council, *Lost Crops of the Incas: Little-Known Plants of the Andes with Promise for Worldwide Cultivation.* (Washington National Academy Press, 1989), p. 153.

[3] Ibid., p. 146.

invaded Mexico five centuries ago found Aztec Indians raising, using, and even worshiping amaranth, which the Aztecs called the "grain of the gods." The Indians fed it to children and others in need of special nutrition and sent thousands of bushels to their emperor as tribute. Warriors prized the grain as a source of energy and strength. In a strategy to subdue the Aztecs, conquistadors wiped out the use of amaranth. Severe penalties were levied for growing or using the grain. Eventually, amaranth vanished from North America almost as completely as the mighty Aztec empire itself.

The strain of amaranth most common to Peru, kiwicha (*Amaranthus caudatus*), contains as much protein as milk. It is high in calcium, phosphorus, iron, potassium, zinc, and Vitamins E and B-complex. Scientists at Pennsylvania's Rodale Research Center—a promoter of organic and low-input agriculture—consider amaranth to be one of the most promising ancient crops. In 1988, researchers evaluated experimental lines in 18 states and four Canadian provinces. Today, amaranth is sold in a wide variety of breads and flours, as well as cereals, pancake mixes, pastas, cookies, snack foods, pastries—and even pilafs. The Peruvian government in recent years has taken a number of steps to encourage   production of the different native grains, including extending tariff benefits for exports and increasing the grains' use in industrial flour. The hope is that the grains might help overcome the chronic malnutrition in the poor parts of Lima and the nation's mountainous rural areas, where as many as half of children less than five years old were malnourished during the 1980s.

However, low yields caused by rudimentary farming methods of Andean farmers make it difficult to meet the renewed demand for the grains. Productivity could soar if fertilizer and better seeds were used and fallow periods were eliminated by rotating the grains with high-yield crops.

To bolster production, an innovative project by the non-profit *Asociación Perú Mujer* is using a twofold approach that coordinates rural grain production with improved marketing in the cities. Supported by a $265,000 loan in 1988 from the IDB's Small Projects Program, the Association is building a grain storage facility in Cuzco to benefit poor farmers who work less than one hectare of land each. Meanwhile, a flour processing plant is planned for Lima. There, the project aims to tap the market among the hundreds of thousands of people from the countryside who have migrated to the sprawling townships of southern Lima. Many have eaten foods made with native grains and would benefit most from their nutritional value. A pilot bakery and processing center started by the Association in Lima in 1983 could not keep up with demand for such products as flour and biscuits.

The project also includes a $90,000 technical assistance grant to help strengthen the Association and train beneficiaries. These investments have helped the group obtain agricultural extension services and instruction in business methods. With that training, poor women farmers are now eligible for credit through the Agricultural Bank of Peru. This breaks the women's former isolation: even the indigenous language that is the sole tongue spoken by the women of Cuzco had kept them out of the economic mainstream.

The women's commitment to the project is strong. Because of Peru's economic problems, the Bank had to delay project disbursements in 1989. By 1990, less than half the loan and its technical assistance funding had been authorized. Nevertheless, the Women's Association continued work on the Cuzco plant, using its own funds and later bridge funding from such international organizations as Save the Children. By mid-1990, the Cuzco plant was 80 percent completed and the association was still continuing its training program in the Lima area.

While it is too early to gauge the results of this project, the start-up has been dynamic, even in the face of the economic and political difficulties straining Peru. With sufficient production and effective marketing, the ancient grains of the Incas could again become important natural resources.

The fuels that run the engine of development are human, financial and technical resources. They ignite the initiative that can make development succeed. These resources strengthen one another. Research yields improvements. Technical assistance brings those improvements to those who need them. Credit and equity investments help turn new approaches into practical reality. The following sections illustrate how these resources influence development.

II

RESOURCES

CREDIT
EQUITY
TECHNICAL ASSISTANCE
RESEARCH AND EXTENSION

CREDIT:
BANKING ON PEOPLE

Nearly one person in three in Latin America lives off the land. The best hope for improving the lives of the rural poor lies in boosting harvests and making farming more efficient.

The seed money to achieve those gains is credit. Financing helps farm families get by from planting until harvest time, buy supplies such as seeds and fertilizer, and upgrade their farms.

Credit is extremely scarce for most poor farmers in Latin America, since they lack land or other assets to secure loans. Sometimes simple innovations in lending—allowing farmers to make payments in-kind or easing loan requirements—can lead to big improvements.

A Long History. Some impediments to farm lending can be traced to the long history of credit in Latin America. Informal financing in the region dates back to pre-Colombian times. Then, lenders used precious metals to make loans and bartered with borrowers for goods and services.

Formal financial activities spread after World War II. As the demand for food grew, new forms of cultivation spread and new lands opened to farming. Along with better roads and communications, modern forms of financing arrived in the countryside. Yet informal lenders still supply most rural credit in Latin America. For example, in Peru, the network of informal lenders, suppliers, middlemen, truckers, and family and friends is believed to be the country's single most important source of farm credit. Only in a few countries, such as Colombia and Costa Rica, have formal means—primarily state banks— penetrated the farm lending system.

Following World War II, many Latin American governments began offering farmers subsidized formal credit. Subsidies were justified to promote agricultural investments; place rural incomes more on par with the rest of the country; achieve socially desirable aims, such as keeping food prices low for city-dwellers; and compensate farmers for adverse effects of macroeconomic policies such as price ceilings, export taxes, and overvalued exchange rates.

Funding for official credit came from domestic savings and foreign sources, including the IDB. New institutions—public agricultural development banks (ADBs)—sprung up to channel funds to the rural sector. Yet the IDB found in 1984 that only 7 to 15 percent of agricultural producers were reached by ADBs; the vast majority of producers continue to depend on fragmented informal markets.

Three decades of evidence have revealed three main problems with ADBs:

• ADB loans are costly in terms of time. Borrowers sometimes must spend hours travelling to and from the bank and filling in forms to obtain loans. In addition, on occasion, borrowers must bribe bank officials to obtain loans. These extra costs especially burden small farmers who are unfamiliar with the lending process.

• Subsidized interest rates have devastated formal financial markets in rural areas. Local private banks could not compete with official institutions at those same rates. The few private banks that existed in rural communities often retreated to cities, where they could earn greater profits. For the rural communities, this meant fewer alternative ways to keep savings. The remaining private banks lent only a small portion of their funds to agricultural projects. Even then, they favored traditional customers, including large farmers and export producers, or less risky short-term investments. Evidence exists that these occurrences have actually increased the inequitable distribution of rural wealth.

• Subsidized interest rates have also held down the profits of publicly supported credit agencies, restricting their ability to make loans, jeopardizing their ability to cover costs, and increasing their reliance on loans and capital from other sources to replenish their capital.

Today, several factors continue to discourage private banks from lending to farmers—much less to small farmers. Farm lending often entails greater risks and costs than financing manufacturing or commercial enterprises. Agricultural production is seasonal and is exposed to uncontrollable factors, such as weather. Bankers must master specialized knowledge of farm production technologies and supervise borrowers closely.

The IDB's Role. In contrast to private banks, the IDB has long considered farm credit to be a promising endeavor. But the IDB cannot afford to lend directly to the millions of individual small-and-medium-sized farmers for their many needs. Instead, the IDB provides global lines of credit by channelling funds through local agricultural or rural development banks. The Bank in effect acts as a money "wholesaler." The IDB then works with money "retailers"—the local banks—to monitor and amortize loans, collect debt, recycle funds, and expand lending to small farmers and their communities. The IDB also searches for ways to make such lending more flexible—yet still profitable.

Global lines of credit have been the largest part of the agricultural loan portfolio of the IDB since it began in 1961, making up more than 40 percent of such lending (see table on page xix). The Bank has helped build and strengthen credit institutions throughout the region. The IDB also has experimented with new forms of credit to help low-income farmers and their communities. The aim is to make credit a tool of agricultural development.

SUCCESS FOR ARGENTINE HONEY PRODUCERS

Talent and energy abound when businesses begin, but cash is often in short supply. For more than 200 cash-strapped young Argentine farmers eager to launch new enterprises and cope with raging inflation, a flexible loan repayment scheme proved vital.

The key to the repayment program was to let the young people repay loans in their crop—honey—rather than cash. The young farmers borrowed funds through the Federation of Cooperative Farm Youth Centers, which since 1950 has worked with thousands of young people in rural areas in the Santa Fe, Córdoba, and Entre Ríos provinces. A 1985 loan from the IDB's Small Projects Program to the Federation helped area producers build a honey-processing plant and honey-extraction centers and install bee hives. Federation members received credit, as well as technical training in producing and extracting honey.

Many of the loan's beneficiaries were the sons and daughters of small farmers. Only one youth in four had completed elementary school, while a mere three percent were high school graduates. Half the farm families lived on less than $1 a day. Financial strains threatened to force young people to leave home to search for work. The new ventures forestalled that. Instead of committing themselves to servicing their debt in the inflation-adjusted local currency (australes), farmers could adjust for unpredictable levels of inflation by using payments-in-kind. Of the 80 kilos of honey they typically produced from a hive each year, farmers set aside 30 kilos to repay their loans.

By 1988, the plant was producing 6,000 kilograms of high-quality honey each day and providing jobs and incomes throughout the area. Honey was marketed in Buenos Aires under the label SANCOR (Santa Fe-Córdoba). Family incomes stabilized—during hard economic times for much of Argentina—and many of the young farmers nearly matched their families' incomes from honey production alone. They paid back the loan, as well: when the project ended in 1990, farmers had paid nearly 171,000 kilograms of honey as in-kind loan payments.

The project marked the first time a payment-in-kind system was used under the Bank's Small Projects Program. Since then, similar systems have been used elsewhere. For example, in Neuquen, Argentina, an IDB-backed project is using payments-in-kind at two different stages. After the project began in 1988, farmers raising angora goats repaid credit with alfalfa they grew to improve the goats' diet and spur breeding. During the project's second stage—production of the goat's long, silky hair to be sold as knitting wool for sweaters—the farmers will have the option to pay back their loans with angora wool.

LIBERALIZING FARM CREDIT IN JAMAICA

Sometimes, a simple key can unlock agricultural credit. Flexibility provided the key in a farm credit program in Jamaica.

In 1983, the IDB approved $10 million to back a line of global agricultural credit. Originally, the program aimed to provide short-, medium-, and long-term credit to about 4,300 small farmers working two to ten acres of land. Those funds provided working capital and backed investments in equipment, livestock, and infrastructure. The loans also supported an innovative program to conserve soil on some 1,880 acres. Terraces, hillside ditches, and drainage canals would be built. Trees would be planted on some 790 acres of new forests.

The program was executed by the Agricultural Credit Bank of Jamaica and the Ministry of Agriculture. The International Fund for Agricultural Development provided another $10 million loan.

At first, funds were disbursed slowly: the program was too rigidly confined to very small farmers in four pilot areas. The original disbursement "pool" was small: only an estimated 86,000 farmers in all of Jamaica farmed plots of two to ten acres. Of these, only 23,000 lived in the four areas originally covered by the project. The situation posed a dilemma for the IDB and its Jamaican counterparts. While the program design helped extend credit to the poorest of the poor, an objective of the program, the difficulty in finding enough creditworthy borrowers jeopardized the program itself. The problem had two solutions. Either the loan could be canceled or the eligibility criteria could be made more flexible. Jamaica's Agricultural Credit Bank and the IDB opted for flexibility.

Thus, the program was opened in 1985 to farmers across the nation. Administrators boosted the size of farms eligible for loans to 25 acres from the previous limit of two to ten acres. In addition, credit regulations were liberalized to permit more farmers to borrow funds.

The changes worked. By the end of 1989, a total of 14,155 loans had been disbursed, benefitting 12,900 small farmers—more than three times the original goal.

STRENGTHENING SELF-HELP EFFORTS IN EL SALVADOR

The "life force" or "backbone"—*fuerzas vivas*—of the city. That's what San Salvador's Mayor José Napoleon Duarte, later president of El Salvador, called the small merchants—mostly women—who sell their wares in San Salvador's markets. Until the early 1970s, that backbone was badly strained.

To buy merchandise from wholesalers, the stall-holders had to tap the informal credit market for funds. Lenders charged exorbitant real terms of interest, ranging from 300 to 600 percent on an annual basis. Those high interest rates kept food prices high.

The merchants found their own solution to the problem. In 1969,

the IDB helped fund construction of the city's first modern central wholesale market and five municipal retail markets. The beautiful new physical set-up of the markets encouraged stall-holders to launch a mutual savings-and-credit association, the *Asociación Cooperativa de Ahorro y Crédito de Vendedores de los Mercados* (ACOVMER) in 1973. The group approached commercial banks for revolving lines-of-credit for working capital. Soon, members obtained short-term credit at an annual equivalent rate of 60 percent, a fraction of the rate they were paying to informal sources.

For some time, the IDB knew nothing about this ingenious way of tapping commercial credit. Then, on a market inspection tour, a Bank official spotted an unmarked door and asked the market manager what lay behind it. "Last year," he explained, "one of the merchants, Señora Pepita Elimira, persuaded me to let her have a tiny janitor's closet, a desk for files, and two chairs. I was so embarrassed to permit this 'unplanned' activity that I did not permit ACOVMER offices to be identified with a sign."

From such modest beginnings, ACOVMER quickly grew. One of its first activities was to organize five nurseries in homes near the market for children between one and four years old. The child care freed the youngsters' mothers to work in the markets and complemented the five nurseries—one for each retail market—built as part of the 1969 IDB market loan. ACOVMER also arranged for food to be sold at a discount to pregnant women and offered cooperative training. And the group obtained credit, legal, and technical assistance by becoming a member of the Salvadoran Institute for Cooperative Development.

ACOVMER continued to branch out. In 1976, it joined a nationwide network of cooperatives. In 1989, it expanded its objectives and goals to receive new members from new markets in the city. It now offers a range of family-oriented services, including scholarships for members' children to attend high schools and universities, life insurance, a retirement fund, family medical insurance, pharmacies, and child care for infants. To help members save money, it created a warehouse that buys products directly from farmers and factories. By eliminating the middleman, the system saves members as much as 40 percent in wholesale costs on their purchases. From its original membership of 93 vendors (all but one of whom were women), ACOVMER by 1989 boasted 625 members, including 225 men.

ACOVMER's success inspired the formation of at least three other vendor associations in El Salvador, including two in Santa Ana and one in Nuevo El Salvador.

ACOVMER's self-help efforts also inspired the IDB. The Bank has integrated steps to help associations of market stall-holders benefit from Bank loans to public markets in Barranquilla, Bogotá, Guatemala City, Medellín, and Quito. The Bank also has added social infrastructure, such as day care centers, to its market loans. In one wholesale market in Bogotá, tenants took their own affairs one step further. In the spirit of ACOVMER, they established an on-site elementary school, building the classrooms themselves and hiring teachers at their own expense.

SPEARHEADING NEW CROPS IN PERU

For as long as local farmers can remember, cotton has been the principal crop of Peru's Ica Valley, south of Lima. But in the early 1980s, Ica farmers began to grow grapes, mangoes, avocados, tomatoes, corn, and asparagus, thanks in part to a new farm credit program.

Asparagus was a major innovation for the valley and Peru, which had never grown the crop before. To make the shift, the Ica Valley learned a new calendar. Farmers targeted production for the November-to-May season, when the Northern Hemisphere was blanketed in winter and could not grow asparagus. The Valley's farmers stepped in to ship high-quality exports.

After being trucked to the Lima international airport 240

kilometers to the north, the crop is flown to Miami, and then on to such cities as New York, Chicago, Philadelphia, Boston, and Los Angeles. During the peak season from November through January, the valley's farmers fill a cargo plane each day.

The shift to asparagus came in the mid-1980s, in the wake of declining cotton prices, rising asparagus prices, spreading cotton plant diseases, and rising cotton production costs. Fausto Robles, director of the Farmers Association of Ica, an influential group of medium-scale producers founded in 1947, led the change. Profit-motivated local farmers quickly joined in.

They found asparagus well-suited to Peru, like other developing countries, because the crop requires considerable labor. However, such labor must be reasonably priced. Taiwan, for example, produced asparagus for a time, but cut production after it lost most of its manpower to better paying jobs in industry.

Robles believes Ica Valley farmers had not grown asparagus earlier in part because of their natural conservatism about switching from traditional crops. Land reform also slowed the switch. Large holdings were broken up, starting in 1969. The cooperatives that replaced them, while large, lacked managerial know-how to carry forth innovations. When mid-sized farms sprang up in the Valley in the 1970s, interest in new crops and new markets awakened. But good management was needed to make the dream of greater profits a reality. Asparagus is not easy to grow. It requires more water than cotton and very clean soil. The Farmers Association of Ica met the challenge. It provided technical assistance to farmers; grew seedlings on its experimental farms; and built an asparagus packing plant and refrigerated warehouse, partly with funding from the *Banco Agrario del Peru*, the country's agricultural bank, and the United States Agency for International Development. The IDB's role came in loans to some 37 Association members to support their crops. The loans were part of an IDB-backed credit program through the *Banco Agrario del Peru* that helped some 6,000 farmers in Peru expand production and buy supplies and equipment.

Today, farmers in the Ica Association produce 2.5 million kilos of asparagus annually for export. Farmers still plant 50 percent of their land in cotton, but they have diversified their crops as never before. Asparagus now covers 1,200 hectares, about 15 percent of the land under cultivation by Association members.

Every innovation needs a leader. Carlos Malatesta was a leader in introducing asparagus to the Ica Valley. Nearing 80 years of age, Malatesta is the dean of the valley's farmers. He had planted all his land in cotton until 1975. Then he began experimenting with other crops, including alfalfa, grapes, marigolds, and pecans. When the option came to plant asparagus, he was especially interested. Loans through IDB-financed credit programs helped him finance the switch. In 1989, he sold his land to a private firm, which planted asparagus on 50 of his original 117 hectares. Señor Malatesta continues his interest in asparagus by working at the local processing and refrigerating plant.

While an innovator, Señor Malatesta also is practical. "There is nothing romantic in this business. You do not plant a crop because your father or grandfather did. You plant to make money."

That lesson has not been lost on other farmers in Peru. Spurred by the success of Ica's farmers, members of at least nine other Peruvian farmer associations have taken to planting asparagus, including farmers in the provinces of Chincha and Nazca, and Canete, Chiclayo, Huarmey, Huaral, Lima, Piura, and Trujillo.

EQUITY: INVESTING IN THE FUTURE

Throughout Latin America, companies are struggling under a burden of debt. Outside investors can help them ease that load. Companies can gain not only money, but valuable know-how, by joining forces with the IDB and foreign and domestic investors.

The IDB increasingly is finding ways to invest directly and indirectly in Latin American businesses and help them structure their operations. The upsurge comes at a time when many Latin American governments, spurred by the economic crisis and other factors, have adopted economic policies anchored in free markets and are showing a greater openness to the external world. By 1990, several countries had liberalized their investment regulations to encourage foreign investment in their economies.

The region also has begun to re-evaluate the role of small- and medium-scale enterprise in creating jobs, providing goods and services, and decentralizing economies (see section on Small Projects, pp. 16-27).

The IDB's Role. Throughout the region, the IDB promotes businesses through direct and indirect investments. The Inter-American Investment Corporation (IIC), which began operations in 1989, functions as an autonomous multilateral investment corporation affiliated with the IDB. The Venezuelan Trust Fund (VTF), a $500 million fund administered by the Bank, has channeled funds to private companies throughout Latin America.

The IIC helps private enterprises—especially small and medium-sized businesses—in three ways. First, it provides credit and capital stock directly or through local financial intermediaries in projects that are financially and economically viable. Second, the Corporation taps the world's capital markets to bring funds to Latin firms through co-financing, syndication, joint investments, and guarantees of subscription to securities or shares. The IIC also offers advice in such areas as privatization and corporate restructuring. Finally, the IIC helps member country governments promote and increase exports. The IIC has capital stock of $200 million contributed by the governments of its 33 member-countries.

The Corporation concentrates on those projects and businesses that will yield adequate returns and that help the development of the Latin American countries where these businesses are based and operate. The IIC believes that only those projects that can stand up in a free market economy will be able to generate sustained profits for the economy of the host countries. Thus, the IIC makes its investments without government guarantees.

To identify sound investments, the Corporation sends missions to Latin countries and responds to requests by businesses. "We wish to base our success on the ability to find quality partners through a unique Latin American network of contacts, made up of nationals of each country who can identify good business opportunities and develop a personal relationship with sponsors," said the IIC's General Manager, Gunther Muller.

In its first full year of operations in 1990, the IIC approved financing totaling $66.6 million for businesses in 12 countries. It is estimated that these investments and loans will create more than 10,000 jobs and generate $164 million in exports. Several of the IIC's financings have been in agriculture-oriented businesses, including:

• An Uruguayan firm that produces fresh fruit for export out-of-season to Europe and Brazil.

• A Chilean firm that is developing a commercial aquaculture facility to cultivate scallops to be sold mainly to markets in North America and Europe.

• A tomato pulp processing plant in northeast Brazil that would help one of the less-developed regions of the country and bring new technology and assistance to small farmers, who would supply the tomatoes.

• An Ecuadoran firm that is building an instant coffee plant in Guayaquil.

As a multilateral institution oriented toward the private sector, the IIC must "start thinking and behaving like a private enterprise,"

General Manager Muller stressed. "This requires that it adopt a set of values, beliefs, and operating modalities that are proper in this sector." The Corporation draws its executive and professional staff entirely from the private sector. It has established contacts with private sector groups in all of its member countries and evaluated markets for its services. The Corporation also has carried out discussions with government officials from various Latin American countries on possible collaboration in the privatization of public enterprises. In addition, the IIC has identified opportunities to restructure private companies and stimulate new flows of external investments into the region. It has conducted studies and considered arrangements to participate in external debt conversions that would tie private sector transactions to reductions in the public debt, particularly intra-Latin American debt.

The Venezuelan Trust Fund. The Fund was launched by Venezuela in 1974 to prime the pumps of Latin America's economic development. As oil revenues flooded Venezuela during the oil boom of the 1970s, the government contributed $500 million to the IDB to launch the Fund. The Fund's Equity Financing Program aided small and medium-sized private companies through the subscription of shares or capital participation in the capital stock of enterprises. By the early 1980s, the VTF was fully disbursed, but revolving funds still are used for export financing, which supports Latin American exporters of capital goods and services. The Equity Financing Program helped the IDB gain valuable experience in private sector financing and helped pave the way for the establishment of the IIC.

NURSING A SICK COMPANY TO HEALTH IN ECUADOR

As a producer and distributor of veterinary products, *El Campo, S.A.* (CAMPOSA) knows what is needed to nurse sick animals back to health. The Ecuadoran firm also knows what it takes to restore a failing company to profitability. In the late 1970s, CAMPOSA was such a failing company itself.

When CAMPOSA opened its doors in 1964, it had big plans for

the future. It would go to its customers, rather than waiting for them to come to it. That brand of active marketing was virtually without precedent in Ecuador. CAMPOSA was one of the nation's first companies to hire traveling salesmen, recalled Nestor Cubillos, one of the firm's founders and its general manager. The company also planned not merely to sell veterinary and agricultural products, but to make them, too.

The company built a main plant in Guayaquil and invested in costly machinery and construction. The projected investments looked reasonable. But in 1973, the energy crisis struck. The project suddenly became an unmanageable drain on CAMPOSA's capital resources. "The most we could have lasted was one more year," Señor Cubillos recalled. "We had effectively lost more than half our capital. We either would have had to liquidate the company or substantially reduce our activities."

Ironically, the same energy crisis that nearly destroyed CAMPOSA indirectly provided its salvation. The rapid rise in petroleum prices in the early 1970s suddenly boosted revenues to oil-producing Venezuela. The nation decided to use some of these funds to establish the Venezuelan Trust Fund (VTF) at the IDB. It allocated $500 million. Some of the new fund's resources were used for equity financing of private companies, such as CAMPOSA.

Through VTF, in 1980, the IDB approved the purchase of $560,000 of the company's stock. Through the IDB, CAMPOSA also found another source of funds: a government agency in the Netherlands, the Financing Corporation for Developing Countries. That agency viewed CAMPOSA as a basically sound company that could play a significant role in Ecuador's development. In 1980, the Dutch agency provided another $360,000 for the purchase of CAMPOSA's stock. Duphar, a Dutch manufacturer of veterinary products, provided technical support for CAMPOSA.

The infusion of capital and support restored CAMPOSA's health and enabled it to grow and become a manufacturer of veterinary and agricultural products. Its product lines grew from 10 to more than 100. Many are under license from international companies such as Cyanamid of the United States, Ciba-Geigy of Switzerland, Coopers of England, and several manufactures of artificial insemination products from France. Its own product line—CAMPEX—has created local employment and carries a larger profit margin. The firm has continually tried to improve local production. CAMPEX line products include not only veterinary products for livestock but also household inspect sprays, disinfectants and cleaners, and flea sprays and vitamins for dogs.

From its initial start with 10 employees, CAMPOSA had grown by its 25th anniversary in 1989 to a major company with 75 employees, sales of almost $1.5 million, and a profit of $185,000. The company now has some 12,500 square meters of buildings, including offices, a laboratory, and a plant for making pesticides and packaging licensed products.

Señor Cubillos reflects on his company's turn-around: "Equity financing brought CAMPOSA more than just monetary benefits. Before, we had a small company that operated in a small way." But working with the IDB and the Dutch agency, CAMPOSA developed new kinds of information about finances and markets. It learned how to launch new products. And it upgraded its efficiency, for instance, by computerizing all its data.

The association with the IDB, which owns 27 percent of CAMPOSA's stock, has also given the firm prestige, according to Señor Cubillos. "The fact that CAMPOSA has as one of its shareholders an institution such as IDB has created a lot of confidence for us in the business community," he said. After the IDB's investment, commercial and development banks reopened their credit lines to CAMPOSA, enabling it to survive its crisis.

NEW USES FOR THE COFFEE BEAN IN COSTA RICA

Subproductos de Café, S.A. (SUCAFESA) was a small Costa Rican company that set out to help solve a big problem in Latin America: what to do with the huge quantities of waste that flow from the manufacture of coffee.

Beans make up less than half the weight of the average coffee berry. The rest is pulp and a jelly-like mucilage. Processors traditionally dump wastes into local rivers, spreading pollution and health hazards.

Each year, the Latin American coffee industry discards about 10 million tons of such waste as it processes more than 17.5 million tons of coffee berries. "We have been producing coffee for 200 years," Kenneth Rivera, SUCAFESA's general manager, noted. "In all that time we never found a solution to the waste problem."

To find an answer, SUCAFESA invested in 10 years of research, starting in 1974. Using a process developed entirely locally, it converted pulp into an energy-rich and nutritious animal feed. The new brand of animal feed was to help Costa Rica curb costly imports and save scarce foreign exchange. SUCAFESA's local product was to be 40 percent cheaper than the imported corn it would replace.

SUCAFESA also came up with a way to separate different chemicals from the discarded pulp for possible resale. Pectin extracted from mucilage could be used as a food emulsifier and to make laxatives, coagulants, plasma, healing compounds, antitoxins, cosmetics, soap, adhesives, plastics, and synthetic fibers. SUCAFESA also worked to develop a method to extract caffeine for use in soft drinks and drugs, and to produce alcohol by fermenting liquid wastes that pour from processed pulp.

SUCAFESA's processing plant in Alajuela Province was the first of its kind in the world, and its scientific findings can be attributed in part to the high proportion of equity funding. This enabled SUCAFESA to channel half the venture share capital to research. Shareholders included the Government of Costa Rica, the Central American Nutrition Institute, and farm cooperatives in Costa Rica. The IDB bought $290,700 of the company's common stock in 1980 through its equity financing program, tapping the Venezuelan Trust Fund. For all its innovative research, however, SUCAFESA was unsuccessful as a business venture in Costa Rica. Far from reaching its goal to process 10,000 tons or one-quarter of the coffee pulp in Costa Rica, SUCAFESA's plant never surpassed the 1,750 tons it processed in 1982-1983. Subsidized corn imported by Costa Rica from the U.S. under the "Food for Peace" program made it difficult for SUCAFESA to compete. Silos where chemicals (such as caffeine) would have been released as the stored pulp fermented were never built. Thus, the processed pulp was unacceptable to farmers as animal feed. By the time SUCAFESA developed its alternative extraction process the firm was bankrupt. The processing plant was closed in 1986.

A study of SUCAFESA by the Bank in 1989 concluded that regardless of its financial problems, the project pioneered a recycling technology that may some day have a positive environmental and economic impact worldwide. For his part, Rivera—who went on to become Costa Rica's Vice Minister of Science and Technology—had envisioned taking the SUCAFESA technology far beyond his own country. If all the waste from coffee towns in Latin America were to be processed, 150 new factories would be needed. This would provide jobs and extend regional development beyond the towns. SUCAFESA had even designed a franchise system to transfer the full range of its technology, from project identification to marketing.

"The day will come when the beverage will be considered a by-product and our healing compounds and animal feeds the real thing," Rivera predicted.

TECHNICAL ASSISTANCE

Sometimes money and resources are not enough to make development efforts flourish. Skills, know-how, and advice also are needed. This is the realm of "technical assistance". This assistance makes resources go further by helping to remove bottlenecks, lowering the cost of carrying out projects, preventing delays, and helping investments succeed. In the long run, such assistance also helps developing nations carry forward their own development schemes long after a particular development endeavor has ended.

Technical assistance has become an almost routine component of the Bank's largest loans, as well as its smallest. More than half of the technical assistance provided by the Bank since its inception has gone to support projects in agriculture, forestry, and fisheries. Such assistance is provided in several forms:

• Strengthening local institutions involved in development. More than 40 percent of IDB technical assistance to agriculture, forestry, and fisheries was of this type through 1988. For instance, in 1989, the Bank helped Ecuador fund consultants with expertise in watershed planning, management, and conservation. Their work will complement $14.5 million in loans to help protect the natural resources of the Paute River basin.

• Identifying good ideas and prospects for investments. For instance, in 1989, in the Dominican Republic, the Bank backed a comprehensive study on the management and conservation of the Bao River basin in the Central Cordillera range. There, the rich ecosystem has been damaged by uncontrolled exploitation. The study, conducted by the Office of National Planning, is expected to lead to a Bank loan to protect the area's renewable natural resources, maintain productivity, and avoid erosion and sedimentation of local reservoirs.

• Helping prepare projects—before the financial assistance arrives. Some 17 percent of IDB technical assistance to agriculture and related activities was of this type through 1988.

• Advising and assisting local people in carrying out Bank-financed projects.

• Linking experts from different Latin American countries. These efforts offer the advantage of lowering costs, improving efficiency, and widening the scope of development endeavors that can be addressed. By working together, Latin nations can find solutions to problems they share. For instance, in 1989, the Bank funded Mexican and Costa Rican specialists to train Haitian officials who are working to develop irrigation and agriculture around Haiti's Blanche River. The project, financed in part by an IDB loan, aims to rehabilitate 3,000 hectares where soil and water resources have deteriorated. Other examples from 1989 show the range of IDB technical assistance activities:

• Training. In Paraguay, a $120,000 technical assistance grant complemented a credit program to help seven agricultural cooperatives serving some 850 indigenous families in the arid Chaco Desert region. The technical assistance will expand training for farmers, strengthen the cooperatives, and help establish the first of four training centers for indigenous women.

• Research. The Bank continued the support it has provided since 1974 to three agricultural research centers in Latin America: the International Center for the Improvement of Maize and Wheat in Mexico; the International Center for Tropical Agriculture in Colombia; and the International Potato Center in Peru. The centers conduct research to improve nutrition, lessen shortfalls in farm output, and increase production of basic foods, such as grain, legumes, tubers, and livestock products.

• Technology transfer. Extension spreads better methods of agriculture, fishing, and forestry. In rural eastern Guatemala, the Bank extended technical assistance and credit to agro-industries and other productive enterprises, as well as to farmers producing such crops as corn, black beans, potatoes, and coffee. The technical assistance was used mainly to strengthen the expertise of the Guatemalan Movement for Rural Reconstruction in project analysis, marketing, and farm credit.

• Technological advancement. Satellite and computer studies survey natural resources and assess patterns of development. In Jamaica, technical assistance to the Government and the Centre for Nuclear Sciences of the University of the West Indies is helping to establish an environmental monitoring and evaluation system. The aid will back efforts to develop an environmental database, analyze maps of polluted areas, and train environmental technicians.

Relative to the Bank's overall lending program, technical assistance programs represent a small portion of the Bank's activities. Only about eight percent of Bank-wide total costs have been devoted to technical assistance. But while the amounts often are small, the effects can be lasting—building a base of knowledge, skills, and experience that can propel development.

LAUNCHING A DAIRY INDUSTRY IN NICARAGUA

Harsh realities can undermine even the best-laid development plans. That's what happened in Nicaragua, in its efforts to build a dairy industry to serve Central America. In the early 1960s, Nicaragua was

flush with success from a breeding program to upgrade the quality of Nicaraguan beef and boost exports. Enjoying a beef surplus, Nicaragua then decided to increase dairy production, too. In 1965, the Nicaraguan government, through the *Instituto de Fomento Nacional de Nicaragua* (INFONAC), an autonomous government agency in charge of the execution of economic development programs, approached the multinational Nestlé company about developing a dairy industry in Nicaragua. The new industry would help cut imports of European powdered milk, create jobs, and save foreign exchange.

To carry out the project, the *Compañía Centroamericana de Productos Lácteos, S.A.* (PROLACSA) was set up. Investors included INFONAC (15 percent), Nestlé (31 percent), *Asociación de Ganaderos* of Nicaragua (11 percent) and private interests from Central American countries. The joint venture was a brilliant and daring concept. Together, the backers launched a plant to produce whole milk powder under Nestlé's Nido and Lirio Blanco labels in Matagalpa in central Nicaragua, an area that has long raised dairy cows. PROLACSA borrowed money from the IDB to conduct a feasibility study, carried out by Nestlé technicians, to build market access roads to Matagalpa and add feeder roads to the planned milk powder plant. In all, some 400 kilometers of roads were built in the area. The plant was the first of its kind in Nicaragua and possibly in all of Central America. It opened in late 1969. To help buy milk processing equipment, the IDB extended an industrial global line of credit to INFONAC. The IDB also provided a line of farm credit, administered by the Agricultural Bank of Nicaragua, to help local farmers produce milk of high enough quality to make Nestlé's powdered whole milk for export.

Nestlé provided the model for establishing the modern enterprise, as well as marketing surveys, valuable trademarks, expertise in engineering, project management, and plant operation, and contacts with suppliers of machinery and other needed components.

Nestlé-backed specialists, including agronomists and veterinarians, helped local farmers produce milk. This task was eased by the relatively small number of farmers—some 120—participating in the project in its early years.

Nestlé's participation also attracted other financing because the company pledged that its subsidiaries throughout Central America would buy all the milk products made in Matagalpa and sell them through their marketing channels. From 1970 to 1979, the milk powder was sold throughout Central America. Guatemala and El Salvador were major customers.

In its first decade, the enterprise performed better than planned and surpassed its production goals. Private Central American investors fully subscribed their shares in PROLACSA. The PROLACSA plant encouraged dairy farmers to increase their herds, improve calving rates, and increase milk yields. Soon, PROLACSA was producing at maximum capacity.

Then, in the late 1970s, Nicaragua's civil war passed through Matagalpa. Most of the dairy cattle were driven to Honduras or slaughtered. PROLACSA was deprived of its source of raw milk and slashed its operations to a fraction of its capacity. Although the plant continued its operations, its market shrank to Nicaragua alone.

That sad occurrence in no way invalidates a splendid concept. A multinational corporation built a vertically integrated agro-enterprise in partnership with the host government and the IDB. Yet the IDB contributed the bulk of its funds indirectly. For its part, the IDB showed how a multinational corporation's production and marketing technologies could help spur development. The project has been used by Harvard Business School as a case study of a joint venture among a multinational business, a development organization, and a host government.

YOUTH CLUBS IN LATIN AMERICA

Throughout Latin America, young people are leaving farms to look for work in cities. Youth clubs modeled after U.S. 4-H Clubs are helping to slow the exodus by adding purpose and hope to young rural lives.

The clubs help young men and women gain valuable expertise in and around the farm and participate in community affairs. Their range of activities is reflected in their Spanish name, 4-S Clubs (*Salud, Saber, Sentimiento y Servicio*), after the U.S. 4-H Clubs (Health, Head, Heart, and Hand).

Carlos Cedeño González knows the value of 4-S training and assistance. He worked full time on his father's 15-acre farm, situated in Costa Rica's state of Cartago, a region of striking beauty, ridged with rugged volcanic mountains, covered with a green mantle of coffee plantations and pastures, and blanketed with fields filled with vegetables and sugar cane.

As a poor young man, Carlos could offer creditors no financial guarantees or security. The 4-S Clubs stepped in to help. The groups had initiated a credit program, thanks to a grant from the U.S. Kellogg Foundation. When greater funding was needed, the IDB on two occasions provided $500,000. The Bank also provided technical assistance grants to train leaders of the 4-S program and support the organization.

Costa Rica's National 4-S Club Foundation lent Carlos $500, tapping funds from the IDB's Small Project Program. That first small loan enabled him to buy fertilizer, seed potatoes, and insecticides. Then Carlos persuaded his father to let him farm a few acres of the family holding. Drawing on training he received from his 4-S Club and the

local extension agent of the Ministry of Agriculture, Carlos carefully prepared his hillside plot by hand and planted potatoes. Five months later, Carlos hired young people to help harvest the crop. With proceeds from that first harvest, Carlos not only paid off his loan, but cleared a couple of thousand dollars. With his proceeds, he took out a second loan. He planted more land, refined his techniques, and after selling his crops, had $8,000 in the bank. Now a fullfledged entrepreneur, Carlos was to learn the costs, as well as the benefits, of taking business risks. His 1984 investment in potatoes lost money: he is working hard to recoup his losses.

Another young businessman is Rafael Fallas Ureña. Rafael has big responsibilities: his father is dead. To support his family, he also paints houses. In 1979, he received a loan of about $600 from the 4-S Club to buy bees and bee hives. During his first year of operations, he earned a net profit of about $900 by selling honey. He invested some $500 of this sum in a honey extractor and materials for a shed that he built to store his bee-keeping equipment. A second loan helped him expand further.

Olman Serrano and his brother Rolando have long-range plans for their 4-S credit of $2000. In 1979, they used the loan to buy avocado tree seedlings on two hectares of hillside land. They grafted buds from their father's adult avocado trees onto each seedling to cut three years off the time it will take the trees to begin bearing fruit.

As the Serranos are showing, one benefit of the program is to introduce improved farming techniques to adults in the region. The 4-S Club method has also spread far beyond Costa Rica. Within a few years after the program had begun, Costa Rican social workers lent their services to a private foundation in Argentina to help establish a program of 4-S clubs there. And the IDB, through the Small Projects Program, has supported 4-S Clubs in five other countries: Colombia, the Dominican Republic, Ecuador, Jamaica, and Panama.

In Panama, the credit helps students in agricultural high schools put their lessons to the practical test by funding actual farming ventures. In Ecuador, club members must take a week-long seminar, learning facts such as the water requirements of cattle, before they can receive credit through the IDB-backed program. The Bank backed a $90,000 grant for the training program. Once projects are underway, the youth must keep meticulous records of their expenditures. By spreading such skills along with credit, the program is helping young people help themselves—one of the ultimate goals of development.

RESEARCH AND EXTENSION

In the 1940s, in the fields of Mexico, the seeds of an agricultural research system were sown—a system that has changed the world. From those first halting experiments to boost yields of wheat has grown an international network of researchers that is feeding the world.

That research launched the "Green Revolution", the amazing advances in yields in wheat, rice, and other cereal crops that banished the specter of worldwide hunger. Today, researchers face a potentially greater challenge. With world population poised to mushroom from five to seven billion people in the next 20 years, it has become paramount not only to achieve worldwide food security, but to sustain the environment and the natural resources involved in producing the extra food.

Latin America is part of the solution. The region hosts three of the 13 international agricultural research centers (IARCs) that discover and spread advances in the production of food crops to the developing world. The International Center for Tropical Agriculture (CIAT) in Colombia concentrates on improving agriculture and crops grown in the lowland tropics of Latin America, including rice, beans, cassava as well as forages and pasture. Potatoes are the focus of the International Potato Center in Peru (see vignette, p. 60). Improving maize, wheat, barley, and the hybrid triticale are the areas of concentration for the International Maize and Wheat Improvement Center (CIMMYT) in Mexico.

All three centers work under an umbrella group, the Consultative Group on International Agricultural Research (CGIAR), a voluntary association of 40 donors, the IDB among them. The Bank's initial technical assistance grant to CGIAR in 1974 marked the first time it had ever financed agricultural research, much less on a global scale. Since then, gains stemming from the research system have made foodstuffs more abundant and profitable throughout Latin America and the developing world—the biggest impact the Bank has received for its development dollar, bar none. Today, the IDB's cumulative contribution of $124 million to CGIAR represents more than one-quarter of its total agricultural technical assistance grants.

Latin America is also home to two major national research centers: Argentina's National Agricultural Technology Institute and Brazil's Agricultural Research Corporation (see vignette, p. 58). These centers focus on areas of domestic concern, including improvements in export crops such as soybeans and coffee.

In addition, regional centers and research networks for Central America, the Southern Cone and the Andean countries have also spread gains. The IDB has provided long-term financial support to these international, regional, and national research efforts directly and through the IARCs. As a result, a generation of researchers is carrying advances forward. By the mid-1980s, roughly half the professionals in agricultural research in Latin America had obtained some training at IARCs. From 1985 to 1989, another 4,200 professionals participated in IARC training courses.

The Bank has promoted the sharing of technological advances among the countries of the region by providing the seed financing for two agriculture research and technology networks: PROCISUR (Argentina, Bolivia, Brazil, Paraguay and Uruguay) and PROCIANDINO

(Bolivia, Colombia, Ecuador, Peru and Venezuela). The networks assign and coordinate research projects among the countries under the technical supervision of the Inter-American Institute for Cooperation on Agriculture (IICA).

Highlights of Latin America's Research System. Among the most impressive gains borne of agricultural research have been:
• Greatly increased yields in beans, corn, rice, potatoes, and wheat. These staples make up half of calories of the typical Latin American diet. Yields for these crops rose dramatically from the 1970s to the mid-1980s. Much of this success can be traced to high-yielding, short-straw grain varieties. Their spread has been rapid and wide. By 1983, more than half the wheat and rice grown in Latin America was of this type. Increases in output have brought benefits of some $1.5 billion each year.

• Strengthened resistance of crops to pests and improved tolerance to unfavorable soil or water conditions. These gains have extended the areas where crops can be grown, reduced post-harvest losses, cut the costs of chemical pesticides, and led to new markets and uses for improved varieties.

• Increases in exports of traditional export crops, including sugar, coffee, and bananas. High-yielding varieties of sugar that resist major local diseases have been developed. The spread of higher-yielding varieties of coffee has reduced the pressure to open new land and helped keep Brazil the world's largest coffee exporter. The widespread adaptation of disease-resistant varieties of bananas helped Ecuador, Central America, and the Caribbean increase their share of exports.

• Mechanization, particularly the use of tractors, has led to greatly expanded agricultural frontiers, especially in Brazil, Venezuela, and Central America, and increased productivity of irrigated areas, especially in Mexico. These changes laid the groundwork for biological and chemical innovations that boosted food production in the 1970s.

New Challenges. Even greater advances are needed in the future to feed a growing and increasingly urbanized population. Despite the triumphs of agricultural research in Latin America, the region has turned from a net exporter to a net importer of food. Civil and political strife, unfavorable government policies, changes in world markets, the debt crisis, and variations in climate—all have taken a toll on farm output and income. The traditional answer to increasing food supplies has been to open new land to farming. However, this option is no longer practical in wide areas. Farmers in Latin America and throughout the developing world have increasingly moved onto marginal, environmentally fragile land. Moreover, settlement is often politically and economically costly and socially disruptive. New food supplies must come from increases in productivity. Research can yield those gains.

But agricultural researchers must make environmental sustainability a centerpiece of their efforts. The CGIAR's Technical Advisory Committee supports this shift in emphasis and recommends almost doubling the amount of research the IARCs devote to managing and conserving natural resources.

Increasingly, research centers will have to act as facilitators— adopting the research flowing from their own research and from other major research institutions and helping developing countries translate these into more food production in stable agricultural systems.

This task is particularly important because agricultural research has become more difficult. The gains that were so stunning for wheat, rice, and other cereals cannot be expected to spread to many other crops after only a decade of systematic research. Unlike cereals, these are not grown under homogenous or large-scale conditions, are not as easily stored and transported, and lack well-established distribution systems. Even so, impressive gains in yields and outputs of cassava, beans, potatoes, and tropical pastures have already occurred. Production has been helped by better varieties and disease-free plants, improved cultivation, and better storage techniques. Location-specific varieties need to be created.

Challenges include helping small-scale farmers boost and maintain production on difficult soils and in fragile ecosystems, spreading strains that resist disease and tolerate stress, and continuing to improve yields. These tasks may be helped by new biotechnological methods to develop plants, which promise to speed research and cut development costs.

Domestic research capabilities must be strengthened to complement work in other countries that share similar geo-climatic conditions. Such sharing accounts for many of the gains in agricultural productivity that Latin America enjoyed in the 1970s and 1980s. For instance, Honduras' own research and extension work in beans helped it adapt a virus-tolerant line of beans from Guatemala. Thanks to a collaborative system of bean research launched by CIAT in Central America and the Caribbean, a network of agricultural institutes in ten countries could test beans for tolerance to a major scourge, the golden mosaic virus.

Future gains in agricultural productivity will depend upon perfecting technology to succeed with particular natural environments and institutional frameworks, adjusting policies appropriately to support new technologies, and investing in sound physical and institutional infrastructure.

Effective research also requires careful management. In particular, national institutions must be able to absorb the assistance of international and regional groups. Some Latin American countries, particularly Argentina and Brazil, have built up high levels of scientific capability. But many national institutes have been constrained by the lack of stable levels of annual funding to pay salaries and other operating costs. Momentum was lost in the 1980s, when the region's economic crisis caused large cutbacks in operating budgets for research and extension services. Research and extension activities often require ten or more years to show significant results. Their long-term nature makes it important to secure financial support and establish clear-cut criteria by which to judge performance.

The activities also require new funding mechanisms. Most extension services have been provided at public expense. Yet experience shows that charging fees to large and medium-size producers can be a feasible—and desirable—way to recover costs fully in some cases. A useful precedent for ways that privatization can be introduced into both research and extension work is provided by the regional consortia of livestock farmers in Argentina, Uruguay, and Paraguay. Imaginative efforts are needed to identify ways that private companies, government services, cooperatives, farmer associations, non-governmental organizations and international donors can work together to spur research and diffuse results.

The IDB is taking a new approach in its support of international agricultural research. In the past, Bank funds have financed the core budgets of IARCs. Starting in 1990, however, the Bank has funded the preparation of special programs targeted to the specific needs of IDB member countries, primarily in the area of applied research and training. From 1990 to 1994, about 60 percent of the Bank's contributions to the international centers will finance these special programs. The balance will provide budgetary support. In another change, the Bank has stipulated that up to 10 percent of its funding can be used for special programs that are important to the region, but which are conducted by centers outside of Latin America.

BRAZIL'S NATIONAL RESEARCH INSTITUTE

From its lush tropical forests to its vast plains, Brazil seems to be an agricultural cornucopia. But the reality is more complex. Hunger still plagues Brazil. And protecting the environment is central to Brazil's agricultural future. Tapping Brazil's agricultural abundance—while safeguarding the environment and increasing farmers' profits—is the work of Brazil's national research agency, the Brazilian Corporation for Agricultural Research, *Empresa Brasileira de Pesquisa Agropecuaria* (EMBRAPA).

A semi-autonomous institution within the Ministry of Agriculture, EMBRAPA began operations in 1973 and today supports research activities in a network of 21 centers throughout Brazil. In the years following creation of EMBRAPA, Brazil quadrupled funding for agricultural research and got big results.

The agency's emphasis is on the practical. It develops and refines methods and technology that farmers and others can readily use and that reduce farmers' risk. It concentrates on the nation's most crucial agricultural products: beans, corn, dairy, livestock, rice, rubber, soybeans, and wheat. And it focuses on key agricultural areas: the *cerrados*, the vast pasturelands and savannas primarily in the states of Goiás, Minas Gerais and Mato Grosso; the semi-arid areas in the northeast; the humid-tropical regions in the north; and the fertile areas of the south.

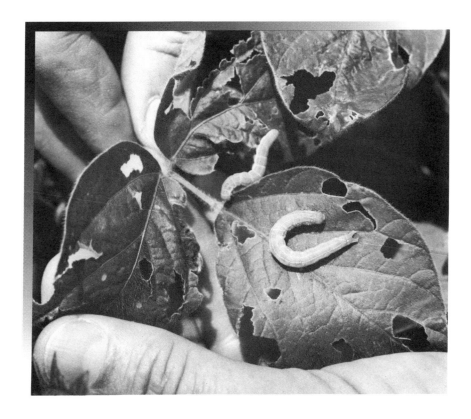

EMBRAPA's applied research has yielded impressive gains. For instance, Brazilian farmers have doubled soybean production in 15 years, thanks in part to breakthroughs in agricultural research by EMBRAPA. Soybeans have replaced coffee as Brazil's top agricultural export, and Brazil now accounts for a quarter of all soybeans produced worldwide, second only to the United States. Equally important, Brazil has been able to keep production costs below those of U.S. soybean farmers.

EMBRAPA's emphasis on harnessing the forces of nature to increase soil fertility and combat pests has helped soybean farmers avoid massive applications of chemical fertilizers and pesticides, which are costly and environmentally harmful. EMBRAPA pinpointed the types of bacteria that were most efficient in converting nitrogen from the air into a form that soybean plants can use. This discovery has saved farmers some $1 billion a year in nitrogen fertilizer costs and has helped keep Brazilian producers competitive on world markets. Researchers have also enlisted nature's aid in fighting insect pests. One of the two main pests that attacks soybeans is the velvet bean caterpillar. A virus was found to be a natural enemy of the caterpillar. Researchers at EMBRAPA's National Soybean Research Center isolated the virus and mixed it with clay powder. Farmers mix the powder with water and spray it on their crops. A small packet of powder, costing about $1—as much as 75 percent less than chemical applications—can treat one hectare. Farmers can save even more money by making their own powder by collecting and grinding up caterpillars killed by the virus. In 1988, this method was used on six percent of Brazil's soybean crop, saving the country an estimated $43 million. Moreover, it does not add toxic chemicals to the environment.

EMBRAPA has worked to improve other crops, including a thornless blackberry bush and new varieties of pears, citrus fruit, and currants. At its National Institute for Cotton Research at Campina Grande in Paraíba, researchers have improved pest management systems and the yield and varieties of cotton, also an important crop in Brazil.

Results like these—and the promise of future research—have warranted the IDB's continued support. In 1976, the Bank loaned EMBRAPA $66.4 million to train manpower and work in such areas as genetic resources, soil survey and conservation techniques, production of basic seeds, and improvements in production systems in several parts of the country. In 1984, the Bank extended a follow-up loan of $70.8 million to EMBRAPA to build new facilities, buy equipment, and train staff. A third loan, under negotiation in 1991, would further support EMBRAPA's efforts to modernize agricultural technology in Brazil.

POTATO RESEARCH IN PERU

Among the diverse and bountiful crops planted by the Indians of the Andes for thousands of years, only the potato has become a worldwide food. Unknown outside the region until the Spanish conquistadors arrived in the 1500s, the potato today is the fourth largest food crop on the planet, grown in about 130 of the world's nearly 170 independent countries.[4] One year's crop is worth more than $100 billion.

Now, this ancient crop is the subject of some of Latin America's most modern research. Researchers have returned to the ancestral home of the potato in the Peruvian Andes to study and improve this vital food. The results are spreading around the world.

At the International Potato Center (CIP) near Lima—one of three international agricultural research centers in Latin America—scientists are developing potato varieties that will be cheaper to use, more resistant to disease, and more productive per area of land.

Among the Center's chief successes is the development of true potato seed. For millennia, farmers have planted the tubers themselves—a cumbersome process. A full metric ton of potatoes is needed to plant one hectare of land. But the same job can be done with a handful of seeds.

Yet seeds present drawbacks. They, too, are labor intensive to plant and are not yet economical for commercial growers. CIP researchers are working to overcome this problem. Scientists also are investigating ways to improve seeds, for example, by making them more resistant to disease.

CIP has advanced a simple but amazingly effective way to increase potato yields—by storing seed potatoes in natural diffused light, instead of in complete darkness. This method lengthens the storage period, reduces storage losses, cuts sprout elongation, and increases the number of sprouts. Seeds retain vigor and more of them are produced, boosting yields. And farmers gain flexibility in deciding when to plant their potato crop: they can try to time their harvest for the weeks when prices are high. The technique has spread rapidly from country to country and is being widely promoted by government agencies.

Throughout the developing world, potatoes are grown with methods that have not changed much over the centuries. Changing those methods requires changing farmers' attitudes and time-honored ways. Thus, CIP researchers pay particular attention to farmers. The Center

---

[4] Ibid., p. 94.

has prepared a battery of manuals and materials for trainers who work directly with farmers. The materials are designed for practical use, not to be put up on a shelf. To bring lessons to the field, "traveling teachers" from the Center are distributing and explaining how to plant new varieties of the potato, with yields up to 300 percent higher than those currently in use.

The hub of CIP's activities is the collection, evaluation, and distribution of germplasm. CIP stores germplasm of 90 percent of all cultivated potato varieties. This living resource is at the disposal of potato growers around the world.

Collecting rare potato varieties is a special emphasis of the Center, which maintains a World Potato Collection with more than 13,000 specimens from throughout Latin America. The work has taken on urgency as extinction threatens species. Increasingly, the natural habitat of potatoes is destroyed as land is cleared for pastures or converted to other uses. Moreover, farmers are abandoning their traditional varieties for newer strains.

CIP researchers search high and low for germplasm. In 1981, for instance, after 10 years of futile attempts, a little known and endangered species was finally found: several ripe berries were collected. That same year, a rare species considered extinct was rediscovered in a remote spot in the department of Cuzco.

The uses of the World Potato Collection are wide. For example, researchers are using the germplasm to develop plants with genetic resistance to pests, which then are incorporated into integrated pest management strategies.

As of 1989, 23 developing countries had released more than 60 CIP-related potato varieties. National researchers in more than 50 countries were evaluating CIP-bred potato lines, which combine resistance to the most important potato diseases.

The Center also has developed culture techniques for obtaining healthy and uniform varieties of tubers. Other activities include research to control parasites and insects that damage potatoes and to develop varieties that can withstand extremes of hot and cold. Work is also being done to improve potato storage methods. And a new generation of researchers is being trained at the Center.

In a historical context, the work of CIP continues a tradition of potato research in the Andes that dates back some 8,000 years, when hunter-gatherers in the high valleys are believed to have first unearthed and eaten the tuber. Through the centuries, farmers in the region have always carefully selected the specific type of potato best suited to local needs and conditions, which vary considerably in the Andes. The Incas developed freeze-drying to preserve potatoes and distribute them through their empire. Present-day Andean farmers sometimes grow up to 200 different kinds of potatoes in a single field. Following the same tradition of production and research that has brought the potato through the ages, CIP works to spread the potato's success.

Entrepreneurship motivates much development and behind-the-scenes resources facilitate it. But the stage where the drama of rural development is acted out is the countryside.

There, development takes many shapes. Land and water resources may be adjusted. The basic units of rural life—families, homesteads, and schools—may be supported. The basic livelihood of farming and rearing of livestock may be strengthened. The following sections present some of the many forms of rural development.

RURAL DEVELOPMENT

IRRIGATION
INTEGRATED RURAL DEVELOPMENT
AND SETTLEMENT
LIVESTOCK AND ANIMAL HEALTH

IRRIGATION

The well-spring of life is water. Dependable supplies of water, the product of sound irrigation and drainage programs, have brought dramatic improvements to Latin America. Farmers and their communities have been protected from the harsh extremes of nature by lengthening the growing cycle, opening dry areas to farming, and curtailing flooding. Irrigation also insured the success of the "Green Revolution" that brought huge advances in the production of wheat, rice, and other cereals. These high-yielding crops thrive best only if they receive reliable supplies of water at specific times during their growing cycle. In many areas, these conditions are possible only with irrigation.

Irrigation also has opened up otherwise marginal or unproductive lands in Latin America. Irrigated agriculture is the only viable form of agriculture in some areas, such as the Andean regions of Argentina, parts of central and southern Brazil, the valleys of central Chile, northwestern Mexico, and the Peruvian coast. In Chile, Mexico, and Peru, irrigated farming accounts for more than half the gross value of agricultural output.

Irrigation has helped farmers diversify crops in Argentina, Bolivia, Brazil, Chile, Costa Rica, Peru, and Uruguay. Such diversification has helped farmers boost incomes and spread risk. And modern irrigation schemes have encouraged other innovations, such as the use of tractors, which increase productivity.

Among the most far-reaching effects of irrigation schemes is the empowerment of beneficiaries. For example, Mexican farmers forged a truly binational industry with their U.S. counterparts to market their fruits and vegetables in United States and Canada (see vignette, p. 70). For thousands of small farmers, IDB-backed crop diversification schemes have brought the benefits of training, credit, and land titling (see p. 75).

For all its advantages, irrigation is no panacea. Decades of experience testify to the problems of siltation, salination, and poor drainage that have accompanied many irrigation projects. Sometimes, huge investments have been left to crumble because of improper maintenance and support. Latin America is entering a new era in irrigation, promoting the more efficient use of existing infrastructure by rehabilitating projects already in place and completing unfinished irrigation works.

For example, an irrigation system built in the 1950s in Haiti's Artibonite River Valley is now being rehabilitated and expanded. The valley is of enormous agricultural and economic importance to Haiti, covering half the nation's land and accounting for 75 percent of national rice production. Financed in part with IDB loans totaling $34 million, the project includes reconstruction, cleaning and maintenance of existing canals and other parts of the system, construction of secondary irrigation works, loans and extension services for valley farmers, and institutional support to Haiti's Artibonite Valley Development Agency.

The approach of the Artibonite Valley project and similar endeavors has been necessary in part because of the economic problems facing the region, which make it difficult to fund new large-scale projects. Investments already made in existing projects often yield higher and quicker returns than those in new schemes. Moreover, environmental considerations are tempering development.

In addition, many of the easiest investments, close to beneficiaries, already have been made. Some 15 million hectares in Latin America are already under irrigation. Unfortunately, although Latin America is blessed with abundant water resources, much of that water lies far from population and farming centers. Four major rivers—the Amazon, Orinoco, Rio de la Plata, and Grijalva Usmacinta—account for more than two-thirds of the region's total run-off. Yet their watersheds, which drain nearly half of Latin America's land area, are home to only 10 percent of its population—a classic dilemma of distribution that has a costly solution.

To make the best use of irrigation projects that are built, the IDB and other backers have learned to integrate related subprograms into their irrigation investments, such as credit, training, land reform and marketing support to farmers, and research tailored to specific locales.

AN UNEXPECTED HARVEST IN GUATEMALA

In the 1960s, Guatemala had high hopes for irrigation. The nation secured a $6 million loan from the IDB to criss-cross drought-prone areas in southern and eastern Guatemala with a network of irrigation canals. The loan also backed credit and extension services for farmers and training for Guatemalan institutions responsible for irrigation services.

The project was the first of its kind in Guatemala and—as often happens with new endeavors—implementation fell short of goals. The initial plan to build 30 irrigation works was cut in half. Completion was two-and-one-half years late. A follow-up evaluation by the Bank in 1980 reported that barely half the 12,000-hectare project area had been effectively irrigated. Although the project reached out to farmers through extension services, farmers made little apparent progress in using the irrigation works properly and diversifying their crops: they did not shift to higher-valued crops, except for tobacco. "From the perspective of the country as a whole," the evaluation concluded, "the project was not successful."

In 1986, Guatemala requested a follow-up loan. Not surprisingly, that proposal sparked little enthusiasm—not, that is, until officials from the Guatemalan government and the IDB visited the site of the earlier project. What they found amazed them.

Farmers—at their own initiative and at their own pace—had learned to use the irrigation works. Fourteen of the fifteen irrigation works, covering 80 percent of the project area, were operating properly. Farmers who had long planted only once a year were planting as often as four times annually. A new crop—broccoli—had replaced tobacco as the main crop for export. Farmers raised summer crops of cucumbers, melons, snowpeas, and tomatoes. In winter, they planted corn and beans. Middlemen and exporters regularly came to the area to buy the produce.

"This project has brought a lot of money to this area," said one farmer in Laguna de Hoyo in southern Guatemala. "The people used to be much poorer," he added, gesturing to a valley dotted with farmhouses and filled with irrigated fields of broccoli as far as the eye could see. "The houses you're looking at now weren't here."

Encouraged by the farmers' own initiative, the IDB approved a second irrigation loan—backing a smaller and simpler operation—in 1988. With the loan, farmers can build on the success they brought forth from the thirsty Guatemalan land.

EMPOWERING FARMERS IN MEXICO

For U.S. and Canadian consumers, fresh fruits and vegetables shipped from Mexico in the cold of winter are a luxury. For the Mexican farmers who grew them, the distribution system that evolved to ship their produce is their livelihood.

Mexican farmers began with high-value commodities—tomatoes, melons, peppers, and other crops—that could be shipped in the winter and spring to U.S. and Canadian markets, helping to satisfy the growing year-round demand for fresh produce. The fruits and vegetables are grown on land watered by seven massive irrigation schemes launched in 12 western Mexican states in the 1960s. The IDB backed those projects with more than $126 million.

With much foresight, some beneficiaries of the newly available irrigation water realized that stabilizing the export trade in winter fruits and vegetables would be in their best interest. Northwest Mexico, particularly the state of Sinaloa, is especially well-suited for the trade in fresh winter fruits and vegetables. The area lies close to U.S. markets; has inexpensive land, rare freezes, and low wages; and is criss-crossed with irrigation systems.

In 1961, farmers established the National Union of Produce Growers (*Unión Nacional de Productores de Hortalizas*, or UNPH) to link Mexican producers and U.S. distributors. By 1970, Mexican producers owned their own distributorship in Nogales, Arizona, which became their most important border crossing to the vast North American market. There, quality and health inspection procedures became routine and effective.

From 1968 to 1978, Mexican exports of tomatoes, cucumbers, eggplant, and green peppers to the U.S. more than doubled. In Sinaloa, vegetables accounted for as much as 55 percent of the total value of agricultural production, even though they were planted on only 5 percent of the cultivated land. Half the Arizona distributorships were acquired by Mexican producers, most of whom belonged to UNPH. Mexican producer-distributors have since played a major role in the U.S. market for winter fresh fruits and vegetables.

The system that evolved spans the full range of production, processing, and marketing. Farm suppliers, storage operators, processors, wholesalers, and retailers work together. A binational, vertically integrated commodities trade has sprung up. By the 1980s, an estimated 250,000 Mexicans were employed in fresh winter vegetable production, with some 70,000 working in tomato production alone.

Over the years, UNPH professional staff—including agronomists, irrigation engineers, economists, extension agents, and lawyers—have become increasingly skilled. UNPH lawyers learned to lobby the U.S. legislative, executive, and judiciary system. They effectively fought a flurry of measures brought by Florida growers to protect the U.S. market from Mexican imports. Those U.S. complaints, which commenced in 1969, culminated in charges that Mexican farmers were "dumping" their produce at unfairly low prices. Almost a decade and a half later, UNPH and Mexico won the so-called "Tomato Wars" with a ruling that allowed them to continue their tomato exports into the U.S.

Meanwhile, UNPH has succeeded in stabilizing its export trade to the lucrative North American market. The empowerment of beneficiaries of publicly funded irrigation projects has been a major—if little noted—achievement of IDB-backed investments. The IDB has adapted such irrigation and agricultural export-promotion strategies in other Latin American countries, including Argentina, Bolivia, Brazil, Chile, Costa Rica, Guatemala, Peru, and Uruguay.

IRD AND SETTLEMENT: FIGHTING RURAL POVERTY

Uprooting rural poverty poses especially difficult and complex tasks. Rural productivity must be raised to boost incomes. Basic infrastructure, such as electricity and running water, must be provided. Social services, such as education, are needed. Change must occur at a rate and in such a way as to harmonize with the environment and the time-honored ways of rural life.

To root out poverty in the Latin American countryside, the IDB has used two major approaches. The most widely adopted, integrated rural development (IRD), aims to lift an entire region out of poverty. The second approach, settlement, recognizes that poverty moves with people as they seek to improve their fortunes. Settlement programs target for improvements newly settled areas or regions that have long attracted the poor.

Both IRD and settlement programs provide communities with an array of social services and infrastructure, along with measures to boost productivity. The programs' sweep often has been ambitious. For instance, IRD projects have provided assistance in agricultural extension, marketing, education, and health care. Financing, including credit, has been furnished. Basic infrastructure, such as irrigation schemes, water supply systems, roads, crop storage facilities, and housing, has been supplied.

Increasingly important to both approaches have been steps to boost the productivity of the rural poor. Over time, the IRD approach has been refined into integrated agricultural development to concentrate on improving farming, the industry central to rural areas' economic and social well-being. The IDB's settlement projects have come to concentrate on areas where agricultural production could be sustained and settlers would have a reasonable chance of succeeding.

The deeply rooted problems of rural poverty and the urgency and ambitiousness of anti-poverty investments led the IDB to scale back investments in settlement and IRD programs, alike. Each provides excellent examples of how the Bank has evolved through trial and error.

The Evolution of IRD Programs. IRD programs gained favor when the international development community was looking to rural development to help solve two major global problems: the urban explosion and what at the time was believed to be an impending world food crisis. Improving conditions in the countryside, it was believed, would give people the incentive to stay where they were. And small farmers, who tend to specialize in the production of domestically consumed foodstuffs, were believed to have an important role in stemming the threatened global shortage of food.

IRD programs sprang up throughout Latin America. By the mid-1980s, rural development projects accounted for 40 percent of concessional external capital commitments to Latin American agriculture, the highest proportion among the world's developing regions.

By the 1980s, support for IRD schemes had begun to wane. Problems were created by the programs' scale and complexity. The timetable—four to five years until completion—often proved overly ambitious. Coordination proved troublesome. IRD projects tended to stretch government manpower resources beyond their capacity. The commercial goals of IRDs often have fallen short when marketing has been short-changed.

Moreover, beneficiaries often have not been sufficiently involved. IRD schemes have tended to overlook many rural dwellers, including women, the backbone of the rural economy. The majority of rural poor—including landless laborers, artisans, and share-croppers—have tended to benefit directly only from projects' social components, as well as general improvements in the rural economy.

By the late 1980s, it had become clear—through informal observations and a few formal project evaluations—that heavy government intervention, along the lines of massive IRD projects, was not going to lessen inequities and ease poverty in rural areas significantly. Financial resources and costly technical expertise could reach only small target areas. The economic crisis of the 1980s strengthened pressure to turn away from governments and toward free market approaches to solve economic problems. Incentives for individual farmers to boost productivity seemed more likely to spur the economy than massive efforts focused on resolving the complex and difficult problems of the rural poor. By the 1980s, the pendulum of development fashion had started to swing toward systematically generating and effectively managing irrigation and drainage systems, continuing the "Green Revolution" to boost agricultural yields, and promoting effective marketing.

Multilateral financial agencies such as the IDB played an important role in inducing government officials to accept innovations in the IRD approach throughout Latin America. The Bank has limited its support of IRD programs, except under a more flexible and comprehensive system of components and implementation.

Reshaping Settlement Programs. Like IRD activities, settlement programs have been the product of trial and error. They too, often have a wide sweep and were born of urgency. Settlement can be a far-flung, disorderly process. Often, colonists bound for the frontier do not wait until roads and other infrastructure projects are ready. Instead, they spontaneously invade empty or mostly empty land and indiscriminately clear natural vegetation. Governments throughout Latin America must cope with vast, haphazardly colonized areas, where settlers are barely able to scratch out a living and gravely damage the environment in their scramble to survive. The classic example is the opening of the tropical rain forest in the Amazon Basin.

Meanwhile, the amount of good land that can be settled in the region has nearly been exhausted, and government settlement programs themselves have been controversial at best. A 1973 evaluation of existing settlement schemes in Latin America, financed by the IDB and conducted by Resources for the Future, an environmental research organization, concluded: "A number of efforts in the planned transfer of population to new tropical lands have resulted in total failure or stagnation. What attracts and what repels migrants is very imperfectly understood."[5] From its survey of 24 projects dating back to 1950, the

---

[5] Michael Nelson, *The Development of Tropical Lands: Policy Issues in Latin America*. (Baltimore: Published for Resources for the Future by Johns Hopkins University Press, 1973), p. 55.

evaluation reported that project objectives were often unclear. "The real motives—an alternative to agrarian reform, or territorial sovereignty, or unemployment, or the exploitation of idle resources to accelerate economic growth—are difficult to discern."

Over time, the IDB decided its best course would be to help consolidate existing colonization and land settlement projects in areas where agricultural production could be sustained and settlers would have a reasonable chance of succeeding. To sustain development in those areas, environmental safeguards are becoming integral parts of IDB-backed settlement investments.

LAND TITLING IN PARAGUAY

The year 1984 is one Augusto Achinelli Rolón, a dairy farmer in the Department of Paraguarí in central Paraguay, will long remember. That's when he took control of his farmland, thanks to a flexible land titling and farm credit program.

Achinelli began working 13 hectares of land along the highway leading to the town of Paraguarí in 1969. He could not afford to buy the land. So he paid previous occupants for improvements they had made, including leveling the land, digging a water well, and installing fencing. Such informal transactions of untitled land were common in Paraguarí and throughout Paraguay.

Achinelli used half of the land for dairy production and the rest for crops. Like farmers everywhere, he needed credit to plant crops, improve the land, and increase his herds. But he could not get a loan because the bank required collateral—and he did not own the land that could serve as collateral.

His prospects dramatically improved in 1984, when he bought title to the land from the government through an integrated rural development program supported by the IDB. The program allowed Achinelli to pay in annual installments and stipulated only that he farm all of his land. Most importantly, land ownership provided him with an immediate and tangible advantage also offered under the program: the ability to get a loan. At the same time he received his land title, the dairy farmer received the first check for a loan to improve his

dairy operations. He bought more dairy cows and his business expanded.

Achinelli is one of thousands of farmers in Paraguarí who received land titles or small loans under the integrated rural development program. It was designed to boost production of farmers, industrial workers and craftsman, provide extension services and training, and back improvements in market access roads, rural electricity, education and health. The IDB approved a $27.5 million loan for the program in 1981. The International Fund for Agricultural Development (IFAD) extended $3.9 million in co-financing.

The program represented a departure from the Government of Paragay's focus on newly settled areas to a concerted effort to improve titling and other problems in long-standing settlements. Paraguarí, in the densely populated central region of Paraguay, is the oldest settled area in the country. The area traditionally has contributed to the migration to new settlements and to metropolitan Asunción. Because the Paraguarí region presents many of the rural problems characteristic of the central subregion as a whole, the program offers valuable insights into similar efforts in the future.

By the end of 1988, the project was virtually complete. Some 668 kilometers of roads had been built and 26 schools completed. Twenty communities had received electricity. Some 1,500 farmers received land titles and more than 3,000 obtained credit for their small farming operations. To Achinelli and many of his fellow farmers, a title and a loan made all the difference. "I was born a farmer," he said. "All I want is good milk production, a healthy herd and a good pasture."

INVOLVING BRAZIL'S POOR IN RURAL DEVELOPMENT[6]

Key to the success of a farmers' assistance program in Brazil was the active involvement of the rural poor. The project also demonstrated the broad impact of a well-conceived and well-run integrated rural development program.

The program, called PRORURAL, helped 61 municipalities in a poor and underdeveloped area in the southern state of Paraná. The project area covered a third of the state, some 65,000 square kilometers, including some of Brazil's oldest settled areas dating to the 16th century. The area's residents earned, on average, less than a dollar a day.

Residents knew what they needed to improve their lives—and PRORURAL's backers were wise enough to follow residents' suggestions. Faced with limited resources, residents had to set priorities. They made their own choice: they decided first to build roads, then health centers, and finally schools.

Administration improved with the active participation of beneficiaries. For instance, a small farmer who wanted to raise black bass borrowed funds through PRORURAL. He built ponds and diverted "spent" water to a 1,000 watt power generator, which provided his farm with electricity. He also bought the generator with PRORURAL credit, even though credit regulations did not specify such a purchase. IDB encouraged such flexible loan arrangements.

In all, some 85,000 small farmers and their families benefited from the program, which included 14 interrelated activities in agricultural production and research, education, health, infrastructure development, and land registry and surveying. In 1980, the IDB provided

---

[6] This section is adapted from "PRORURAL: A Lesson in Multilateral Lending," *International Herald Tribune*. Paris, France. January 27, 1986.

$80 million of the total cost of $213 million; the Paraná state government and *Banco do Brasil* furnished the rest.

Even a partial list of PRORURAL's achievements shows the breadth of integrated rural development:

• More than 3,700 land titles covering more than 101,000 hectares were issued.

• Almost 36,000 hectares were reforested.

• More than $32 million of credit was extended to small farmers.

• Twenty-one warehouses were built, to be operated primarily by the producers themselves through regional cooperatives and associations.

• More than 5,300 kilometers of roads were built or improved.

• Seventy-one water systems were built in rural communities.

• Eight markets and a marketing pavilion were established for 6,000 small farmers operating through production associations.

• Soil was prepared, graded, and cleared, and dams covering more than 226,000 hectares were built.

• More than 530 schools were built or improved, making possible the attendance of more than 63,000 new students in rural elementary schools; also, 1,825 teachers were trained.

• Nearly 290 rural health facilities and one hospital were built.

PRORURAL's impact is clear to the Association of Farmers of Tijucas do Sulan (AFTS), an impoverished community in the State of Paraná, southwest of São Paulo. Its 130 members are subsistence farmers, selling only the occasional surplus. Only a handful of members use tractors; the rest plow with horses. They grow rice, corn, beans, oats, potatoes, and soybeans.

"For me, personally, PRORURAL has been my salvation", said Antenor Batista da Rocha, AFTS president. "Until it brought us the health post in the village, I didn't have any peace. As one of the very few people with a car, I was always taking people to the nearest hospital, which was 100 kilometers away. [Now] we've got new roads, grain storage facilities, and, what for me is most important of all, schools. Before PRORURAL, it was no use to work hard and produce a large surplus of rice or beans, because there was nowhere to store it. The roads were so bad that you often could not get to market."

AFTS members also responded enthusiastically to new opportunities offered by the program. "When we suggested that they build fish ponds to supplement their diet and sell another product in the market, we were a little bit cautious at first," said Audalio Teixeira de Lima, a PRORURAL agronomist who provided AFTS with technical assistance. "We thought that they might be suspicious of such an innovative technology. [But] the response was fantastic."

Despite the success and enthusiasm PRORURAL generated, the project had its share of problems. It should have been finished by Spring 1986, but completion was postponed until January, 1987. The Paraná state government, pressed for funds, reduced the program's funding. Then, plans for a four-year $250 million follow-up project financed in part with a $100 million loan from the IDB were abandoned because the State of Paraná faced a financial crisis. Ironically, the same integrated approach to development that helped the project succeed also marked it as too ambitious an undertaking during the tightening economic conditions of the 1990s.

CONSOLIDATING COLONIES IN PARAGUAY

When the great Itaipú dam was built along Paraguay's border with Brazil, the region faced a flood of workers. During construction, the entrepôt city close to Iguazú Falls, Puerto Presidente Stroessner[7], housed as many as 20,000 temporary workers and their families and was growing in population five times faster than the rest of the country. The challenge that faced Paraguay was to manage the dispersal as construction on the dam and hydroelectric plants wound down.

The unemployed labor force faced a choice. They could leave for other opportunities, remain and settle along the Paraná River, or try to farm in the rural settlements that spontaneously dotted the Departments of Alto Paraná and Canindeyú.

To consolidate 15 of these settlements, the IDB approved a $14.1 million loan in 1980. The project funded new roads enabling the new farmers to market their products, ten rural schools to serve 29,000

---

[7] Renamed "Ciudad del Este" in 1989.

children, two health centers, and two health posts. Land titling was provided to 2,390 plots and credit extended to new landowners.

The big unknown was how sustain farming on the frontier. Technology suited to small settlers at that locale was needed. The IDB's project design called for setting up a model farm and tree nursery to provide trees for reforestation and experiments with new crops and plant varieties. Findings were to be given to extension agents, who would incorporate them into production plans for settlers who applied for agricultural credit. To receive credit, settlers would have to follow approved forest-clearing and cropping practices, join a local commodity committee that jointly marketed surplus products such as soybeans, cotton, and corn, and reforest areas needed to curb soil erosion. Experts worked both in field stations and settlements.

This modest and ultimately unsuccessful effort to integrate environmental concerns into a settlement program would be considered far from adequate by today's standards, when the Bank's Environmental Protection Division evaluates all projects for environmental impact. But for a project design begun in the 1970s, the concept was innovative.

Equally innovative was the land titling program run by the Government of Paraguay's *Instituto de Bienestar Rural* (IBR), South America's oldest public agrarian reform agency. Land titles could be issued once settlers paid the first installment of 20 percent of the price of the land, as assessed by IBR. The land title could serve as collateral for farm credit issued by the *Banco Nacional de Fomento* (BNF), the country's single largest source of agricultural credit. This simple, innovative, and generous provision made it possible to issue 2,710 titles, nearly 1,000 more than originally planned by IBR. The Bank made 1,500 loans totalling $6.35 million, or some $4,230 per loan.

Festive ceremonies often accompanied the issuing of land titles. On these occasions, farmers exhibited their produce and shared views about the program's progress with visiting government officials. A lively exchange of valuable information ensued.

As the need to boost foreign exchange earnings grew, BNF shifted the priority for its loans from local food staples toward export crops, such as soybeans and cotton. The Bank also favored local wheat, which was to substitute for wheat traditionally imported from Argentina.

BNF's supervised credit mechanism, through which extension services were provided by the Paraguayan Ministry of Agriculture, made it relatively easy to introduce new crops among farmers in the 15 settlements. Over time, this innovative settlement consolidation program showed success in land titling, credit, education, market access roads, and health—all critical in a region that by the 1980s had swelled to a population of more than 209,000 people[8]. But the environment protection schemes proved disappointing. Settlers, pressed for cash income, were hard put to conserve soil through reforestation. From 1982 to 1987, while cultivated land in the area increased 39 percent annually, enabling poor farmers to subsist on their new lands, the rate of deforestation was 67 percent. Cleared land was devoted to annual cash crops without any sound soil conservation scheme.

The IDB is searching for credit and other mechanisms to spur environmental protection while balancing the other pressing needs of settlers that were met so successfully by the project in Paraguay.

RAISING HEALTHY LIVESTOCK

Ever since the discovery and conquest of the New World, livestock has been integral to the society and economy of Latin America and the Caribbean. Columbus brought the first cattle to the hemisphere on his second voyage to the New World in 1493, landing on the island of Hispaniola. As conquest proceeded from island to island and then on to the mainland, settlements were always secured by a base of cattle. By the mid-1500s, large herds were already roaming the pampas of the Southern Cone states of Argentina, Chile, Paraguay, and Uruguay. Later, the armies for national independence led by the great liberator Simon Bolivar were financed and fed with cattle herds from his native Venezuela.[9]

Yet, livestock as a key industry grew slowly. At first, cattle and

---

[8] Population of the Department of Alto Paraná, which includes Ciudad del Este.
[9] John E. Rouse, *The Criollo: Spanish Cattle in the Americas.* (Norman: University of Oklahoma Press, 1989).

sheep were killed for their hides. Well into the 19th century, meat had little value: carcasses were left to rot. That changed with the arrival of refrigerated ships in the 1880s. Brazil and the Southern Cone states became prime suppliers of frozen beef and mutton to the United Kingdom and parts of Western Europe. Wool exports also soared. As rural populations grew, ranchers and farmers competed for land. Fences arose across pastures. Ranchers improved pastures and introduced superior breeds to increase productivity.

By the 1980s, Latin America had more than 16 percent of the world's livestock, exported nearly one-quarter of the world's beef, and earned $1.9 billion yearly from livestock exports. At the same time, however, imports of livestock products, mainly highly subsidized dairy products from developed countries, were soaring. At current rates, Latin America could become a net importer of livestock products in the 1990s, if dairy imports do not slow.

An Important Sector. Better livestock management could spur great improvements in the regional economy. Livestock represents one of the few ways that small farmers can save and invest. Increased productivity would create jobs in rural areas, as well as cities, where industries such as tanneries and shoe-making are major employers. A growing livestock sector could slow the massive influx of agricultural workers into already overcrowded cities. Moreover, the livestock industry holds high potential for improving Latin American diets and incomes.

Yet production remains well below the levels the region should enjoy. The area's plentiful pastures give it a comparative advantage in livestock production that is yet to be fully developed.

Productivity could be increased through better breeding and feeding, as well as investments in basic infrastructure, such as roads and electricity. Small producers could compete better with large operations by complementing crop production with cattle raising.

Improvements in animal health also are needed. About 160 major animal diseases afflict the region, increasing animal morbidity and mortality, slowing animal growth, curbing fertility, and striking hard at exports. Producers lose ten percent of the value of their herds through disease.

Although Latin America is making strides to control animal disease and much has been accomplished, more remains to be done in introducing new technology and training field workers to help with epidemiological surveillance. Latin America's ministries of agriculture need to make animal health activities a higher priority. Such projects have suffered as governments have cut spending to cope with high debt—a serious problem when a successful first stage of a program could not proceed to later stages. In some cases, the strict fulfillment of immunization and control goals has been overemphasized, at the expense of fully conceptualizing both animal health problems and their origins.

Other Challenges. The challenges to improving the livestock sector are many. Government policies—such as export taxes, subsidies, and price controls—have hampered livestock production, as has direct government intervention in livestock processing and marketing. Moreover, governments have offered little assistance to the private sector to increase production and productivity. These policies are changing.

In addition, little international livestock research has occurred in Latin America—in contrast to the work on corn, wheat, potatoes, and tropical crops underway at the region's three international agricultural research centers (see p. 53). An exception is the Tropical Pastures Program of the International Center for Tropical Agriculture (CIAT) in Cali, Colombia, where work is underway to improve livestock production in grassland areas such as Colombia's Llanos Orientales. CIAT is developing and promoting technology to improve pasture lands with marginal acid soils in order both to increase livestock production and conserve tropical soil resources.

Latin American producers also face fluctuations in demand and prices for exports. Developed countries have cut imports, consuming less beef for health reasons and protecting their own domestic production. Disease also has cut demand for exports of fresh Latin American beef. And exports have shifted toward lower-value processed beef sought by fast food markets in Western Europe and North America, a growing market.

Throughout Latin America, beef remains the meat of choice. Only high prices would discourage consumption. However, rising beef prices—and inexpensive feed—would encourage diversification to more efficient forms of production, including poultry, pork and fish.

Environmental and Sociological Considerations. The time-honored activity of raising livestock has drawn sharp criticism as it has spread to the Amazon basin. As that area has been cleared for pasture, concern has mounted that the activity harms rainforests and that livestock production cannot be sustained as fragile soil loses fertility, hardens, and erodes. While recent research suggests that problems of soil fertility, structure, and drainage apparently can be managed with known technology, it should be noted that in most of the Amazon basin, livestock development was not very profitable at prices prevailing in the 1980s. Other areas—including the drylands (*cerrado*) of Brazil and the savannas (*llanos*) of Colombia and Venezuela—are more profitable, pose fewer ecological problems, are less remote and closer to population centers, and require less investment for development.

Critics of the livestock industry also argue that speculators use cattle ranches to obtain and control large tracts of land, displacing indigenous peoples and small farmers. Moreover, increased urbanization has left less land for grazing and places further pressure on proper land use.

The IDB's Role. The IDB views livestock development and animal health as a comprehensive process that surpasses merely the improvement of commercial production. It includes planning for the proper use of appropriate soils for grazing lands; environmental safeguards to protect against indiscriminate clearing of forests for pastureland; and regional integration among countries to better control animal diseases that cross national borders. The IDB:

• Provides technical assistance to help ranchers plan, design, implement, and operate IDB-backed investments.

• Offers marketing assistance and aid to strengthen livestock product processing facilities.

• Helps develop livestock marketing infrastructure, such as roads and bridges.

• Aids national research activities to alleviate the major causes of low livestock productivity.

• Strengthens agricultural credit institutions and public and private livestock institutions, such as agricultural ministries, and cooperatives.

• Channels financing through local intermediaries, including development banks and private sector banks, to help small and medium-sized farmers.

In addition, the IDB encourages governments to remove export taxes and price controls and set positive real interest rates on livestock loans, which promote investments by producers.

The Bank also takes a comprehensive approach toward animal health. The IDB considers investments in animal health to be fundamental not only to combatting a particular disease, but also to improving the means to fight other illnesses in an integrated and organized manner. The IDB helped finance pioneering efforts to improve animal disease-control activities. In the mid-1960s, the Bank concluded that major programs were needed to protect the value of livestock investments. It launched pioneering studies to help formulate bankable projects aimed at curbing or wiping out major animal diseases. In the ensuing years, up to the present, the IDB has supplied some 90 percent of the region's outside financing for animal health programs.

The Bank concentrates on strengthening the infrastructure to prevent and control animal disease, including:

• Training professionals, such as veterinarians and para-professionals.

• Building facilities, such as laboratories to diagnose diseases and factories to make vaccines, antigens, and other medicines.

• Establishing means to monitor the spread of disease, control the movement of diseased animals, and insure the quality and cleanliness of slaughterhouses and meat distribution systems.

• Improving the government administration of animal health campaigns.

A "Cow Condominium" in Mexico

Sometimes, development experts encounter bizarre problems that do not seem to yield reasonable solutions. Supplying fresh milk to Mexico City is a case in point.

In the bad old days in Mexico City and other cities, dairy cows were stabled in cities—and never laid eyes on green pastures. The practice was unhealthy, unpleasant, and dangerous. Major fires swept through Chicago and Manhattan during the late 1800s, when straw ignited in downtown dairy sheds. By the turn of this century, cows were sent packing to the countryside. Milk arrived in the city by refrigerated truck.

Not so in Mexico City. There, the practice of stabling cows in the city continued well into the 1960s. By then, some 700 cow sheds, with nearly 36,000 animals and their fly-infested manure pits, were located in the Mexico City area. Some herds were within blocks of Insurgentes, the city's major boulevard. Milk was sold raw. Nearly half the cows suffered from tuberculosis or other diseases. From time to time, the mass media would focus on the city's antiquated dairy system. No one seemed to know how to end this "scandal."

At first, a legal solution was contemplated. Public health authorities intended to cancel licenses to produce milk in the stables. But this was impractical, because Mexico City had no alternative source of fresh milk.

Milkshed owners volunteered their own solution. In the 1960s, some 17 milkshed owners voluntarily moved north to La Griega, in the State of Querétaro. But profits on their operations were slight, because they had trouble getting locally grown feed and selling small quantities of raw milk to pasteurization plants. Yet their move, and isolated attempts by other dairy producers to relocate, convinced city fathers that a collective or cooperative solution might work.

Inspiration came from California. There, in the lush Central Valley, milk factories flourish with as many as 10,000 cows. These modern facilities supply most of the fresh milk to more than 12 million people in greater Los Angeles, San Francisco, and Sacramento.

Could a variation on the California theme fit Mexico City? Mexican cowshed owners repeatedly visited California to study the U.S.

plants. Several opinion surveys and preliminary studies by Mexico's Ministry of Agriculture indicated that prospects were promising. In 1974, Mexico asked the IDB to help develop a unique "cow condominium." Some 35,000 dairy animals from Mexico City and other locations could be moved there. The Bank expressed interest "in principle" in this challenging proposal and launched several missions to help Mexico develop a program to decentralize Mexico City's milk supply system (*Programa de Decentralización de Cuencas Lecheras*, or PRODEL).

In its first stage, PRODEL moved about 150 stables with 20,000 cows to a village near Tizayuca, about 50 kilometers north of Mexico City. An industrial dairy park was built, complete with a pasteurization and packaging plant, a refrigerated storage area, refrigerated trucks to haul the milk to Mexico City, and a plant to produce animal feed.

A complex was launched to raise calves. For stable holders and their staff, the complex offers family housing, a primary school, centers for adult education, a social hall, sports facilities, a pharmacy, and veterinary services. Altogether, some 7,000 people depend directly or indirectly on the Tizayuca facility. The complex offers such services as marketing, heifer production, and management know-how not available anywhere else in the area.

PRODEL obtains feed from a wholesale feed market. It also contracts for feed from farmers on irrigated lands about 50 kilometers to the north, in Hidalgo, and about 20 kilometers south, in the State of Mexico. IDB contributed about half of the $100 million originally needed to build the Tizayuca complex and its off-shoots.

A series of contracts that guide the complex relationship of the PRODEL entities are a lawyer's paradise and a layperson's nightmare. Nevertheless, by the late 1980s, PRODEL was a well-established, if highly unorthodox, enterprise. A long list of dairy farmers waited to buy a unit in the cow condominium. The state-of-the-art facility has become a popular target for mass media, who want to know how a bizarre idea was transformed into a profitable agro-business complex. A feature article in a 1988 issue of *Cambio* magazine summarized the popular view of PRODEL: "This milkshed is a good child of Mexican agriculture."

ENDING FOOT-AND-MOUTH DISEASE IN CHILE

An ancient scourge—foot-and-mouth disease—is the target of a modern animal health campaign in South America. The disease strikes cattle, sheep, pigs, and goats, weakening South America's livestock industry. While it kills few animals, it greatly cuts meat and milk production and lowers animal birth rates. Exports plunge, because most foreign markets refuse to buy tainted animal products.

Chile was the first country in South America to systematically fight the scourge. The nation was hard-hit. Cattle herds grew a mere 30,000 head between 1955 and 1965. Virtually self-sufficient in beef and dairy products in the early 1940s, Chile was importing some $36 million worth of such products in 1967.

In 1968, Chile obtained the IDB's first animal health loan: $2.3 million. (The entire disease control program eventually cost $90 million.) Chile used IDB funds to help the Agricultural and Livestock Service train personnel, obtain vaccines, buy vehicles, and build technical and administrative facilities. The veterinary service was strengthened to wage a long-term campaign. The government, producers, and the business sector joined forces to tackle the disease.

By 1972, the program was making progress on all fronts: education, disease monitoring, and vaccination. Cattle movements were controlled to contain the disease. The government declared specific areas of the country to be free of the disease.

Sporadic cases still occurred until the late 1970s in cattle imported for local consumption. Finally, in 1979, the last case was reported. In 1981, after the required waiting time of two years, the nation claimed success. Chile declared itself free of foot-and-mouth disease.

However, in 1984, the nation experienced a set-back when an outbreak occurred in Trapa-Trapa, a town in south central Chile. All animals in the area were killed and the outbreak was contained.

Meanwhile, the country maintained close control on its ports, airports, and frontiers. In 1987, Chile became the first country in South America to be recognized as free of foot-and-mouth disease by the U.S. Department of Agriculture. The declaration opened the way for Chile to export cattle and sheep products to the United States, and eventually, to other countries, as well.

Chile has not let down its guard. The virus is extremely easy to transport—even in manure on a traveler's shoe. The nation has enlisted the active support of cattlemen—critical to the program's success. At first skeptical, cattlemen eventually provided great support, not through obligation, but by conviction.

The economic rewards of the program's success have been great. Cattlemen were encouraged to improve their herds and increase production. Chile's animal disease control service has been strengthened to tackle other animal health problems.

IDB has financed similar foot-and-mouth disease control programs in Bolivia, Brazil, Colombia, Ecuador, Paraguay, Peru, Uruguay, and Venezuela. (The disease never has stricken Central America or the Caribbean.) Despite these efforts, and a range of programs backed by other donors and governments, foot-and-mouth disease has yet to be eliminated in any other South American country.

But the institutional structure being developed to combat the affliction is being used to fight other animal diseases. For example, in Bolivia, the Foot-and-Mouth Disease, Rabies, and Brucellosis Control Service (SENARB, after its Spanish name) is reaching more small farmers than ever. The wail of a siren from a government four-wheel drive vehicle alerts farmers in rural areas to bring their livestock to be vaccinated against rabies by the SENARB team. They pay about 60 cents for each animal that is vaccinated—a small price to pay for the peace of mind it will bring. An IDB loan helped SENARB build veterinary service centers and quarantine stalls and buy equipment and vaccines. Thanks to close scrutiny and mandatory vaccination, food-and-mouth disease and brucellosis are generally under control in Bolivia.

CONTROLLING CATTLE TICKS IN MEXICO

Until a few years ago in Mexico's state of Veracruz, most communal farmers, or *ejidatarios*, raised only traditional crops of corn and beans. Very few farmers raised cattle, in part because they had no way to protect their animals from a serious disease called piraplasmosis. Transmitted by a tick, this parasitic disease often kills animals or leaves

them weak, scarred, malnourished, emaciated, and vulnerable to other illnesses. Today, many *ejidatarios* in Veracruz raise cattle—in part because they can now take their animals to public anti-tick cattle dips.

The dips are part of a nation-wide government-backed campaign to rid the country of this tick-borne disease. In 1975, the IDB loaned $35 million loan to Mexico to step up the pace of the program. Some funds were used to build Mexico's National Animal Parasitology Center, train technicians, establish quarantine stations, and buy laboratory equipment. The balance of the loan backed credits to help 175,000 families—organized in associations, cooperatives or other groups—install communal dipping stations and related facilities. In addition, more than 3,300 people, including supervisors and inspectors, were hired to work on the health campaign full-time. The campaign also protected areas free of ticks from the disease.

Under the program, farmers pay a few pesos per head and drive their herds down a passageway leading to a vat. The animals swim eight meters through a weak solution of an organic phosphate insecticide. This kills the ticks. The process is repeated once every few weeks during the high-risk season.

By 1984, the campaign had greatly curbed the disease in Veracruz and other parts of Mexico. Between 1975 and 1984, the percentage of cattle infected with the disease in Mexico fell from 60 percent to 39 percent and annual losses in meat production were cut nearly in half.

More than 35,000 dip stations were built and nearly 100 million head of cattle were inspected.

Despite these successes, efforts to extend the project into southern Mexico in the mid-1980s encountered problems. As the program was expanding into tropical areas, where it is harder to kill cattle ticks, the financial crisis in Mexico forced the government to cut back funding. In Veracruz, however, the program continued. There, it was still commonplace in the late 1980s to see *ejidatarios* herding their animals to a cattle dip.

Similar anti-tick programs backed by the IDB were started in Honduras, Panama, and Uruguay; several other countries in the region run their own programs. It is hoped that an annual vaccine to control cattle ticks may some day replace the chore of regular dipping. Experiments for a new treatment are underway in Australia and East Africa.

Latin America is blessed with dense forests and teeming seas and rivers. Harnessing these rich resources is key to the region's development. But the process of tapping these resources has evolved with the realization that the natural resources of Latin America, like those of the rest of the world, have their limits. The approach is changing from one of "how much and how fast" to careful husbandry for sustainable development. What is needed is a balance to insure that meeting the needs of today's Latin Americans does not compromise the needs of future Latin Americans.

IV

NATURAL RESOURCES

FORESTRY
FISHERIES

FORESTRY

A lush but threatened resource, forests blanket one-third of Latin America—the largest proportion of forest cover on any continent. The region contains about half of the world's tropical forests, most of them in still-undisturbed areas that stretch from the upper Amazon Basin to southern Venezuela and the Guyanas.

Forest resources remain abundant in Latin America as a whole. Yet parts of the region's forests are dwindling as the population grows, cities expand, agriculture and cattle ranching spread, fuelwood gathering intensifies, and commercial timber species are over-exploited. Rapid deforestation, particularly in the closed tropical forests, is a cause for grave concern.

The timeless value of Latin America's forests cannot be overstated. For nearly one of five people in the region, forests provide energy, food, and fodder directly on a daily basis. Forests protect river basins and control soil erosion, which are essential preconditions for hydroelectric production, irrigated agriculture, drinking water supplies, and flood control. They help meet the growing demand for lumber and paper. Forests provide plant and wildlife habitats. They play a role in the regional, and perhaps even the world, hydrological and climatological cycle. They furnish recreational areas for the urban population—and add beauty and wonder to the earth.

Poverty lies at the root of many of the problems plaguing the region's forests. Large areas of Latin American forests go up in smoke each year to make way for farmland. At the same time, demand for fuelwood is growing. Most of the wood consumed in Latin America is burnt as fuel, much of it for heat and cooking for the region's rural population. Firewood consumption has even been rising in Latin American cities—for many rural and low-income people, the energy crisis of the 1970s became a fuelwood crisis in the 1980s and 1990s.

Meeting the challenge of forestry management in Latin America calls for more than technical and financial solutions. People solutions also are needed. A new approach to forestry—community forestry—recognizes that forestry development is not just about trees, but also about people, specifically rural people. Community forestry actively involves local people in meeting their basic needs—food, shelter, fuel, and fodder—through forestry. The approach integrates forestry activities into broader development programs. Community forestry also focuses on activities to improve soil and safeguard the environment, thus increasing agricultural production and improving resource management. To date, social forestry programs have remained small-scale. However, encouraging starts are being made in several countries. Since 1982, the IDB has been developing expertise in community-oriented forestry projects, mostly as components within rural development projects or within the Bank's Small Projects Program (see p. 16).

Sound Commercial Management. Also crucial to the careful development of forest resources are methods of proper commercial management. While millions of hectares of Latin American native forests are burnt and converted to agriculture, only a few areas are managed commercially. Although most all the countries in the region are planting new forests or replanting cleared ones, the ratio of plantation to deforestation on the whole is 1:10—one hectare planted for every 10 hectares deforested.

Among those areas that can be harvested commercially, many of the more accessible forests have been over-exploited, especially the productive coniferous forests in Mexico and Central America and the softwood forests of southern Brazil. Yet overall, Latin American forests are under-managed and under-utilized. Among other things, multiple use products such as fruits, nuts, and resins could be collected from forests for commercial uses.

Plantations established in deforested areas have proven to be economically and ecologically viable investments in the region. Today, plantations provide almost one-third of the region's total annual industrial wood production, although they account for less than one percent of the productive forest area. By the turn of the century, industrial plantations are expected to produce about half the wood used in industry.

Chile illustrates the type of plantation-based forestry development that the region could enjoy. Chile, Brazil and Honduras are the only major Latin American exporters of forestry products that enjoy a favorable trade balance for the sector. Success in Chile has been attributed to low planting costs, rapid growth rates, high volumes, good land transport and harbors, integrated lumber, pulp, and paper operations for domestic and export markets, and substantial public financial incentives for reforestation. More than 90 percent of Chile's wood is harvested from man-made plantations. In the temperate areas of southern Chile, industrial pine plantations support an expanding sawmill and a pulp and paper industry that produces both for domestic and export markets.

Other countries in Latin America, such as Argentina, Brazil, and Uruguay, already earn considerable foreign exchange through sales of forest products based on tree plantations.

In countries such as Costa Rica, which has one of the highest deforestation rates in the world, encouraging commercial forestry could satisfy both the short-term interest in cutting trees and the long-term need to save and manage them. A pioneering program backed by the IDB would provide tax credits to Costa Rican farmers who plant trees. The program would fund the planting of 10,000 hectares of trees on farms throughout the country. However, implementation has been delayed because the precarious financial situation in Costa Rica—as in many Latin American countries—has made it difficult for the government to finance its share of such a large-scale reforestation program.

The IDB's Role. It took years of trial-and-error for the IDB to gear up to promote forestry-related activities effectively in the region. Over time, the Bank has greatly shifted its emphasis in forestry lending. In the 1970s, projects tended to focus on large-scale industrial development, particularly in Argentina, Guyana and Honduras. In the 1980s, the Bank emphasized reforestation and forest management and conservation. The realization that trees, crops, and livestock—when used together—can stabilize land use and boost yields, has prompted innovative agro-forestry management schemes.

Today, the Bank also extends funds to manage other forestry-related renewable resources: soil, water, fauna and flora. New projects finance management of watersheds, urban forestry, conservation of ecosystems, protection of national parks, extension, research, and training, and strengthening institutions. The Bank's efforts aim to conserve and manage forest lands for the well-being of local people and for the socio-economic development of the countries as a whole.

To date, the Bank's forestry-related investment projects have helped to manage and protect some 4.8 million hectares. The reforestation goal of Bank-financed projects amounts to 470,000 hectares.

MANAGING A RIVER WATERSHED IN ECUADOR

When Europeans arrived in Ecuador's Paute watershed at the start of the 16th century, they found the basin blanketed in forest and scrub and dotted with clearings where the Cañaris Indians grew corn, beans, potatoes, and other staples. Little erosion or sedimentation scarred the land.

That all changed with the arrival of settlers and prospectors for precious metals. They appropriated Indian lands and cleared forests for farms. As the newcomers spread, so did soil erosion and sedimentation. In the 19th and early 20th centuries, new roads brought new settlers—and more environmental problems. From deep forest, many areas became sterile wastelands.

Now the area is populated by *campesinos* who work small and uneconomic plots of land on steep hillsides. As their numbers expand, farmers are forced onto marginal lands where they degrade soil until it is depleted. Then they seek new land and repeat the cycle. Silt flows into the reservoir behind the Paute River's hydroelectric plant, reducing its capacity. At current rates, deforestation will completely denude the basin within 30 years.

What can be done to slow this destruction? A project in the region offers wide-ranging answers that could help not only the Paute basin, but other watersheds in Ecuador—and around the world.

The project stemmed from an initial management plan, drawn up in 1978, and from steps in 1982 to establish a National Commission for Watershed Management. From these initiatives, a program to manage and protect about one-half million hectares in the Paute basin emerged. In 1989, the IDB approved two loans totalling $14.5 million for the project. The Bank's loans were among the first investment projects in watershed protection in Latin America. The Bank is also providing a $388,000 technical assistance grant to strengthen the agency that will implement the project, the Ecuadoran Electrification Institute.

Enlisting the support of farmers is central to the plan. Some 40 extension agents will advise farmers on ways to conserve soil, manage pastures, and combine tree plantings with agricultural crops. Some 22,600 hectares are slated for agricultural and agro-forestry extension.

Another 3,400 hectares are earmarked for tree plantations. These will protect soil and provide firewood, fence posts, and other products, reducing the pressure to cut natural forests.

Another 203,000 hectares of non-agricultural land will be set aside in 19 protected areas. There, dikes and retaining walls built along stream banks and waterways will curb erosion. Some 20 forest rangers will oversee the land. In addition, 2,300 hectares of badly degraded land will be protected to help restore natural vegetation and control erosion. Protecting vegetation also will preserve the area's biological diversity, including the year-round cycle of flowering that sustains insects that pollinate farm crops. The feasibility of continuing to dredge the reservoir that serves the Paute hydroelectric plant will be studied.

Overall, the program aims to cut erosion by some 60 percent, preserving soil nutrients and decreasing the need for chemical fertilizers. Fifty thousand small-scale farms in the region stand to benefit from the project, which also aims to extend the useful life of the country's major hydroelectric plant.

Just as important, the project will establish an institutional structure and legal framework that will enable the Ecuadoran government to manage the country's other watersheds, safeguarding their potential for farming, forestry, and hydroelectricity. Overall, the project aims to serve as a model to help other countries manage similar ecosystems. As of 1990, the Bank was financing feasibility studies for similar projects in Colombia, the Dominican Republic, Guatemala, and Honduras.

TREE PLANTATIONS IN ECUADOR

In some spots in the Ecuadoran Andes, trees are so scarce that residents burn manure and straw for fuel—a last ditch practice that harms the environment. Removing straw spreads erosion and eliminating manure robs the soil of potential nutrients.

To relieve pressure on Ecuador's few remaining natural forest stands, an IDB-backed project in the central highlands will use plantations to provide wood for fuel, posts, and particle board.

The project area is owned by Indians who are poor and are not integrated into the national economy. Their interest in reforestation is immediate: to earn cash for planting the trees so that they can buy agricultural inputs and tractors, and, in many cases, make the final payments on their land. As the trees grow, the landowners will extract firewood from thinnings and fallen branches. Residents' children will benefit from harvesting the mature trees.

The plantations will be established by a partly state-owned agency that already operates in the area and whose personnel speak the native Quechua. To plant the trees, the agency will pay landowners or hire farmworker organizations. The agency also will conduct forest research and training. Some 6,000 farm workers will attend two-day courses on reforestation, with audio-visual presentations and field demonstrations. Landowners and the state will share returns from the tree harvests. In this way, the government will recover its financial contribution.

The program will also include experimental plantings of native species. Cypress and eucalyptus will make up the bulk of the plantations. Some native legumes will add vital nitrogen to the soil. To protect agricultural lands, windbreaks of trees will be planted.

In all, the IDB's $6.3 million loan will help establish plantations on some 18,000 hectares of eroding and underutilized communal land. The loan is among a variety of different institutional arrangements and financial incentives that the Bank and Latin American governments are exploring as they find ways to tackle forestry, a relatively new sector for both.

FISHERIES

Bathed by cold South Pacific and Atlantic currents and washed by warm Caribbean waters, Latin America is blessed by highly productive fisheries. The region contains about one-quarter of the world's riches in fish. Using that resource wisely will require good management, sound technology, and careful development.

Latin America is a full participant in the major changes underway in the world's fisheries. Several countries in the region, including Chile, Mexico, and Peru, already compete with developed industrial countries in high seas fishing. Local fishing technology is improving, which may further narrow the competitive gap. The fishing industry also is playing an increasing role in Latin American economic planning, with fishing seen as an increasingly important source of food, as well as a valuable export.

Fish is one of the world's most abundant sources of animal protein. Moreover, many species of fish are relatively inexpensive. As new protein sources from inland and ocean waters, the development of fisheries offer Latin America a chance a strengthen a weak link in its food chain, as well as improve its balance of payments through exports.

Production. Latin American countries reached less than two-thirds their fishery production potential in the 1970s and 1980s: annual catches fluctuated between 10 and 13 million tons. Using existing technologies better, Latin American countries could increase annual catches by seven to eight million tons.

Three distinct fisheries co-exist in Latin America. Small-scale fishing prevails in coastal waters and is important in almost all Latin American countries. The activity requires considerable labor; efficiency depends on the skill of individual fishermen. Coastal fishing communities are gradually organizing into cooperatives, which equip members with modern vessels and gear and help unload, process, and market their catch.

Industrial fishing occurs on the high seas, is capital-intensive, and requires complex and sophisticated vessels. During the last two decades, some Latin American countries' industrial fisheries have progressed rapidly, to the point that they rival other world leaders in efficiency.

A third approach, fish farming, or aquaculture, is beginning to develop in several countries, including Brazil, Ecuador, Chile, Mexico and in the Central American subregion.

In all, fisheries activities employed about two million people in the mid-1980s, mostly in coastal small-scale enterprises.

In southern fisheries, Argentina, Chile, Ecuador, Peru, and Uruguay are the most important Latin American producers. In the northern waters, Mexico is most important. In tropical waters, conditions are favorable for valuable species, such as lobster, shrimp, and snapper.

A New Ocean Regime. The biggest improvements in the region have occurred not in fisheries technology, but in regulating and managing the territory on which fishing occurs. Almost 50 years ago, Chile, Ecuador and Peru were the first countries in the world to establish a common policy and legal system to protect and manage their marine resources. In the 1970s and 1980s, widespread international agreement was reached that coastal nations should have jurisdiction over living resources in an Exclusive Economic Zone (EEZ) that extends 200 miles seaward from the shore baseline, where feasible.

Under the new ocean regime, coastal nations have an opportunity to plan fisheries development against a background of nationally controlled resources. The regime increases each coastal nation's responsibility for harvesting and conserving fishery resources by determining the total allowable catch within each zone.

Environmental Concerns. Sea and coastal resources are afflicted with three main problems. Certain species are being over-fished. Certain areas, especially the Caribbean, are contaminated by petroleum and other wastes. And coastal, beach, and river ecosystems are degrading. As the Latin American and Caribbean Commission on Development and Environment grimly notes, industrial plants and tourist resorts have been established in coastal areas; fishing and farming has expanded; mangrove swamps have been cleared; and arid areas have been mined—all without due consideration to environmental factors or loss of productive potential. These factors are worsened by natural occurrences, such as hurricanes.

In recent years, a number of research projects to evaluate fishing and coastal resources have been supported by several Latin American countries—as well as by such organizations as the IDB, the United Nations Development Programme and the U.N. Food and Agriculture Organization (FAO). The Bank has supported evaluations of the Atlantic coastal waters of Argentina, the Bahamas, the Dominican Republic, Honduras and Uruguay that have studied the volume of biomass, sustainable yield of commercial fishing, and general environmental conditions.

Market Outlook. Latin American fish production has undergone an unprecedented expansion in the past 30 years. Catches have grown fivefold, to more than 15 million tons, from 1960 to the late 1980s. Over time, export products have become more valuable.

Yet hampering greater sales in Latin America are low incomes. For the vast numbers of potential low-income customers, production and marketing technology have not yet made much headway. Indeed, because no ready way exists to market them, fish products such as fish meal are often fed to animals; meat is then sold to high-income consumers.

However, low-income consumers in cities are beginning to benefit from infrastructure—including refrigeration, better transport, and cheaper means to preserve food—that has boosted fish production and improved the distribution of fish in the past 30 years. Interestingly, much of this infrastructure was created to spur exports.

Demand for high-value products such as shrimp will rise as presentation, quality, and distribution of supply improve. Prospects are particularly favorable for shrimp, because some Central and South American countries have natural advantages for raising shrimp through aquaculture. Lower cost production will attract medium-income consumers.

The relatively optimistic outlook for Latin American fisheries must be tempered by the fact that the world catch has been levelling off. Many species that have been eaten traditionally are now fully fished; some varieties are over-fished. However, production could jump if demand increased for unconventional species—such as shrimp-like Antarctic krill, lantern fish, squid, and small deep-sea fish.

Aquaculture. Fish-farming, or aquaculture, can play an important role in coastal and rural development by boosting nutrition among the rural poor, improving incomes, and creating jobs. Moreover, fish farming on a commercial scale does not require high levels of capital investment but is a good earner of foreign exchange. Aquaculture is especially promising at a time when the conventional "capture" approach has reached its limit for several fish stocks in marine and many inland waters.

Aquaculture of fish, crustaceans, and mollusks is expanding all along Latin America's coasts. Some countries stock commercial fish in irrigation systems or man-made lakes connected to hydroelectric projects. Techniques are being developed in most warm water countries of the region to raise tropical species, including *tilapia*, catfish, carp, and local varieties.

Attracted by foreign exchange earnings, private investors and governments have increased interest in raising high-value varieties. Promising cultures include shrimp, trout, and salmon.

Brazil has pioneered fish-farming, with lessons that can boost food supplies and help developing countries worldwide. Fish-farming had been practiced in northeastern Brazil since the late 1940s. In 1979, the Bank approved a $66.4 million loan to back Brazil's first national program to develop its fisheries. The project concentrated on two key components to promote fish-farming: fish hatcheries and training. A series of public hatcheries was built: each was provided with an extension staff to train potential fish farmers, help them prepare credit applications, supervise the project, and market final products. In this way, the extension structure common to conventional agriculture was adapted to fish farming.

Moreover, students from many Latin American countries are studying aquaculture at the vocational aquaculture school in Pirassununga, Brazil. This pioneering school was built with support from the FAO and other donors. The IDB has provided financing for scholarships.

The IDB's Role. In the early 1970s, the Bank began an innovative promotion of both small-scale and industrial fisheries projects. Bank loans are credited with helping boost annual fisheries output in the region by 1.6 million tons. The Bank has strengthened institutions, developed human resources, and supported the private sector at both industrial and small-scale levels through financing and technical assistance.

BIG GAINS FOR MEXICO'S FISHING INDUSTRY

Along Mexico's long coastline, fishermen can point proudly to new boats, villages have gained new jobs, and shops can stock gleaming stacks of fish, all thanks to a massive program to upgrade Mexico's fisheries industry.

Mexico aims to become a major force in the international fisheries trade. And it plans to upgrade Mexican diets through more seafood. Blessed with a rich abundance of fish resources, the nation seeks to make fisheries an anchor of local and national economic development. To meet these goals, the IDB helped Mexico develop a national program to boost its fishing industry—the first such program backed by any multilateral development bank anywhere in the world. The Mexican precedent has been examined by many other countries seeking to net bigger gains from their own fisheries.

During the past 20 years, fishing activity in Mexico has grown from a small-scale program to a large industrialized sector (ranked in the top 20 fish-producing countries in the world and third in Latin America). Among the food-producing sectors of the Mexican economy, this sector has one of the highest growth rates. The IDB has consistently supported and expanded the program over the years. The first IDB loan—$43 million in 1974—backed many firsts for Mexico:

• The first national organization for joint shrimp exports.
• The first national distribution network to market fish products.
• The first trust fund to channel credit to fishing cooperatives to revamp their fleets, and
• The first center to train professional fishermen.

In addition, the program established two national fisheries agencies: the Federal Fisheries Secretariat and the National Fisheries and Ports, which finances investment in the sector. The program also:

• Established a national network of vocational training schools for fishermen.
• Helped diversify production away from Mexico's biggest fisheries export—shrimp—by funding the fishing fleets of other species.
• Fostered fish-farming through research and improved production.
• Strengthened the national network of fishery ports, and
• Pioneered a method to encourage careful management of fisheries. In order to receive credit backed by the IDB, fishermen were required to comply with environmental safeguards that made fishing for some target species ineligible for funding.

Upon the IDB's insistence, some 40 state-owned shrimp-processing plants boosted their marketing clout. They acquired the majority of common stock in the two brokerage firms that controlled sales of shrimp in Mexico's major export market, the United States.

The national fisheries program proceeded in three stages. A second IDB loan of $80 million in 1980 greatly expanded funds to back fisheries operations and make long-term investments. Mexico's fish production during this period doubled, but the economic recession hampered development of the sector and environmental factors became an increasing concern.

IDB channeled credit from the 1980 loan through the National Fishery and Port Bank (*Banco Nacional Pesquero y Portuario*, or BANPESCA). About half the total credit granted to fisheries for working capital from 1983-87 came from BANPESCA's own funds. In addition, BANPESCA, using IDB funds, was practically the sole source of financing for fixed-asset loans. Commercial banks shied away from such lending because they prefer less risky short-term borrowings. The loan also financed work by the *Departamento de Pesca* (DEPES) to improve ports and train fishermen and support personnel.

In 1988, the Mexican Government decided to privatize funding of the huge expansion planned for fisheries and aquaculture. BANPESCA's credit operations were suspended and commercial banks stepped in. This trend is in general agreement with the IDB's current policies in support of sectoral reform and privatization.

The program also worked to husband aquatic resources. The project built on a comprehensive program, drawn up in 1984, to safeguard the environment in Mexico. The National Ecology Program included steps to develop and enhance fisheries and other natural resources. Plans to expand Mexico's catch were linked directly to Mexico's Maximum Sustainable Yield policy. Strong measures were taken to prevent a major decline in fishery stocks because of overfishing. To ensure that activities financed by the program satisfied current environmental regulations, clauses in the Credit Regulations required that all eligible projects show that they would not damage the environment.

By early 1989, Mexico was ready for a third stage of the program, which was included as part of a $140 million loan to Mexico's agricultural sector. The loan supports repair and equipping of tuna and shrimp fleets, construction of processing plants and breeding farms for fish farming, and organization of transportation and marketing networks. Disbursements have proceeded cautiously during the initial period of the loan, primarily because of adverse oceanographic conditions and weak prices for shrimp.

The ups and downs of Mexico's massive fishing development program do not obscure the dramatic breakthroughs that have occurred. From 1968 to 1987, total capture increased almost sixfold, to 1.5 million tons per year. Exports increased more than nine times in value, to $590 million. The number of fisherman tripled to 150,000. Fleets grew to 65,000 vessels. Annual consumption of fish quadrupled to almost 14 kilograms per person. In short, two decades of committed development transformed Mexico's fisheries sector into a major force in the nation's economy and an important part of the Mexican diet.

SMALL FISHERMEN IN CHILE

While Chile boasts a world-class large-scale fishing industry on the high seas, its coastal and inlands fisheries are relatively undeveloped. Their annual catch amounts to less than five percent of Chile's total.

In the early 1980s, an opportunity arose to boost small-scale fishing in Chile. The economy had slowed, export revenues had fallen, and foreign exchange had dried up. In 1982, the IDB lent $189 million to the Chilean Development Corporation (*Corporación de Fomento*, or CORFO) to spur investments in agriculture, industry, mining, tourism, and fishing.

CORFO was designated to lend money directly to firms and channel funds through the nation's commercial banks. But a severe banking crisis and unattractive terms kept banks away. Thus, CORFO placed all the funds directly. CORFO did not consider small-scale fisheries eligible for institutional credit because—like farmers without land titles—they lacked adequate collateral. The IDB sought innovative ways to remove the roadblock to lending.

Chile's National Association of Small Fisherman proposed that loan eligibility criteria be changed to include credit for small-scale fishing activities because they qualified for loan repayment guarantees under a government-sponsored program. CORFO agreed and approved nearly 1,800 such loans. These were used to supply working capital and buy equipment, including boat motors and hulls, fishing nets and gear, compressors, floats and vehicles. The large numbers of motors financed under the program helped fisherman shift from sailboats and row boats, greatly expanding their cruising range.

Loans averaged $7,600, some $400,000 less than typical loans to industrial fisheries. Such small and unprecedented loans challenged many of CORFO's traditional lending procedures. They placed a disproportionate administrative burden on CORFO. And they carried extra risk: their success depended heavily on fishing stocks, which fluctuate, and selling prices, which vary widely.

To meet the challenge, flexibility became the hallmark of the loans. CORFO helped potential borrowers to formulate their own projects. Borrowers retained responsibility for all means of production. These features were critical to experienced small fishermen, who were reluctant to consider loans for equipment based on designs specified by CORFO.

A typical example was Juan Guillermo Quinán, a small fisherman in Valparaíso who used his loan to buy a boat. He conceded the advantages of fiberglass construction—lower maintenance costs and greater durability. But like most other fishermen, Quinán opted for a wooden vessel. The cost was less than half the fiberglass boat and Quinán could do the repairs himself. Also, the wooden boats were more durable when dragged along the sandy or rocky shoreline.

To evaluate loans, CORFO suddenly was called upon to judge market forecasts, catch projections, and operating and other costs. It was impractical for CORFO to acquire its own expertise on these matters. Instead, it tapped existing institutions. The National Fisheries Service helped CORFO advise prospective borrowers, screen loan applications, and follow up with clients after loans were approved.

Most small fishermen were unfamiliar with formal credit instruments. They were accustomed to informal arrangements with middlemen or processing plants, by which they repaid their debt at a discount each time they sold their catch to them. For each approved credit, the borrower had to present collateral, in addition to the capital good.

CORFO tapped the Guarantee Fund for Small Entrepreneurs, which pre-dated CORFO and helped fishermen secure credit without having to offer major assets (which most fishermen did not have) as guarantees. In 1989, the IDB's Operations Evaluation Office (OEO) reviewed the small-scale fisheries program and concluded that too many uncreditworthy fishermen had received loans. Half the loans were overdue by late 1987, in part because CORFO did not have the means to collect payments in the *caletas*, Chile's remote fishing villages. CORFO had initiated legal collection procedures against borrowers. The OEO proposed that loan eligibility criteria be tightened and that collection be improved by:

- Tying repayment schedules to fishing seasons.
- Enlisting other financial intermediaries to accept repayments.
- Delegating responsibility for debt repayment to community leaders, who were respected by close-knit groups of small fisherman and their families.
- Adding incentives—such as a partial rebate on interest—for good community repayment performance.

A management manual prepared by the OEO to help appraise small-scale fishing operations identified species under stress, the fishing of which should not financed, and encouraged fishing for under-utilized species.

Overall, CORFO and the IDB considered the pilot project to fund small-scale fishing promising, despite the problems. The Bank backed further operations in a second global loan to CORFO in 1987, but changes were made to assure loan repayments. A $10,000 minimum loan amount was established and, later, loans were channeled through commercial banks instead of provided directly to the fishermen.

The lessons of Chile's learning-by-doing experience increasingly are being shared with other Latin American countries that seek to develop small-scale fisheries, including Brazil, El Salvador, Mexico and Peru. The IDB's support of small fishermen has become an integral part of its work "to be the bank of Latin America's informal sector," as declared by Bank President Enrique Iglesias.

FRANK MEISSNER was an agricultural economist, an author, a frequent lecturer and teacher, and in his own words, "a pathological optimist". Born in Czechoslovakia, he escaped the Nazis in 1939 and went to Denmark to learn farming in preparation for going to a kibbutz in what was then Palestine. He never fulfilled his original goal of settling in Israel. Instead, he came to the United States, where he earned a doctorate in agricultural economics from Cornell University. His first job was teaching vocational agriculture to World War II veterans, but he also taught at the University of California, California State University, the U.S. Department of Agriculture Graduate School, and at American University.

In addition to academe, Frank Meissner's career included consultancies, private enterprise and international civil service. At the Inter-American Development Bank, where he worked from 1969-1988, he created the Agricultural Marketing Section. After retiring, he continued to work for the IDB as a consultant until shortly before his death on January 19, 1990.

Dr. Meissner's specialty in agricultural marketing was the vehicle through which he carried out his main mission—to help improve food distribution in developing countries. Through his work, his teaching and his writing, he looked for ways to teach people new skills, how to better market their products, and improve their lives. This came naturally to a man who had triumphed over the odds several times in his own life. Frank Meissner embraced life with gusto. He was always ready to try something new, accept failure along with success, and look for ways to do it better the next time.

NANCY MORRISON is a writer, reporter and editor. She has written for the *San Jose Mercury News* and *Congressional Quarterly* as well as for the World Bank, the European Community, the National Geographic Society, and the Bretton Woods Committee. She is a contributing author of *Entangling Alliances: How the Third World Shapes Our Lives* (1990). Her reporting assignments have taken her to Turkey, Indonesia, Japan, Kenya and Europe. She has masters degrees in management from Yale University and in journalism from Stanford University. She lives with her husband and her daughter in Washington, D.C.